PRECIOUS OBJECTS

CHARLES MINTZ

WWW.PRECIOUS-OBJECTS.COM

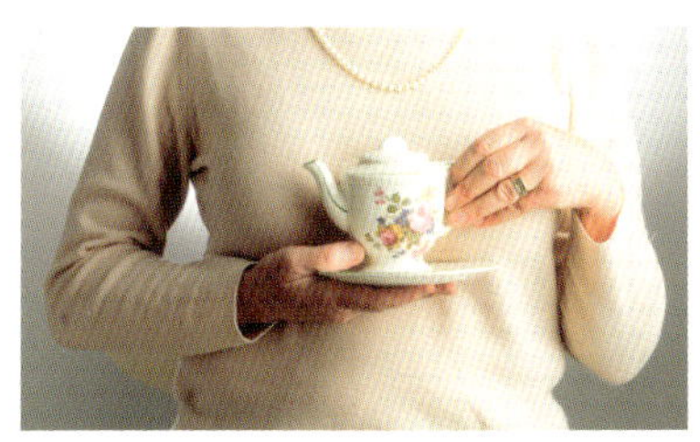

"Things you have had a long time...

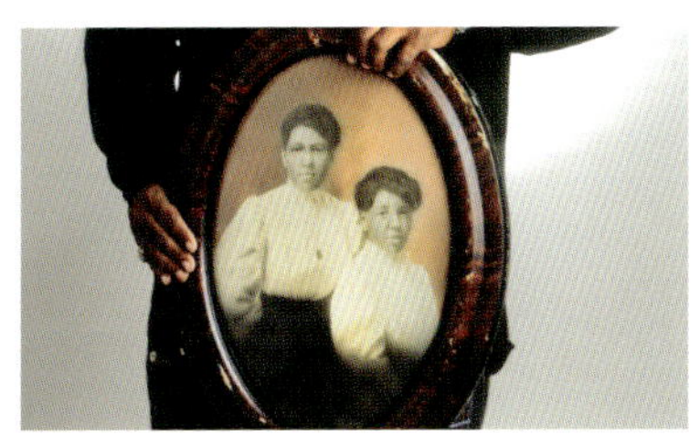

...that have special meaning...

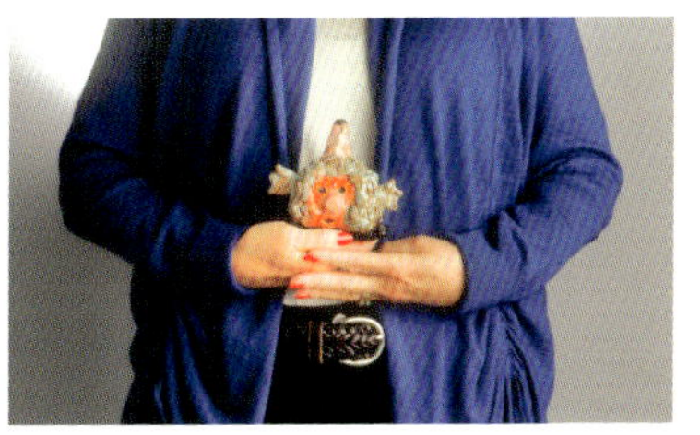

...that you would not or could not replace if you lost them."

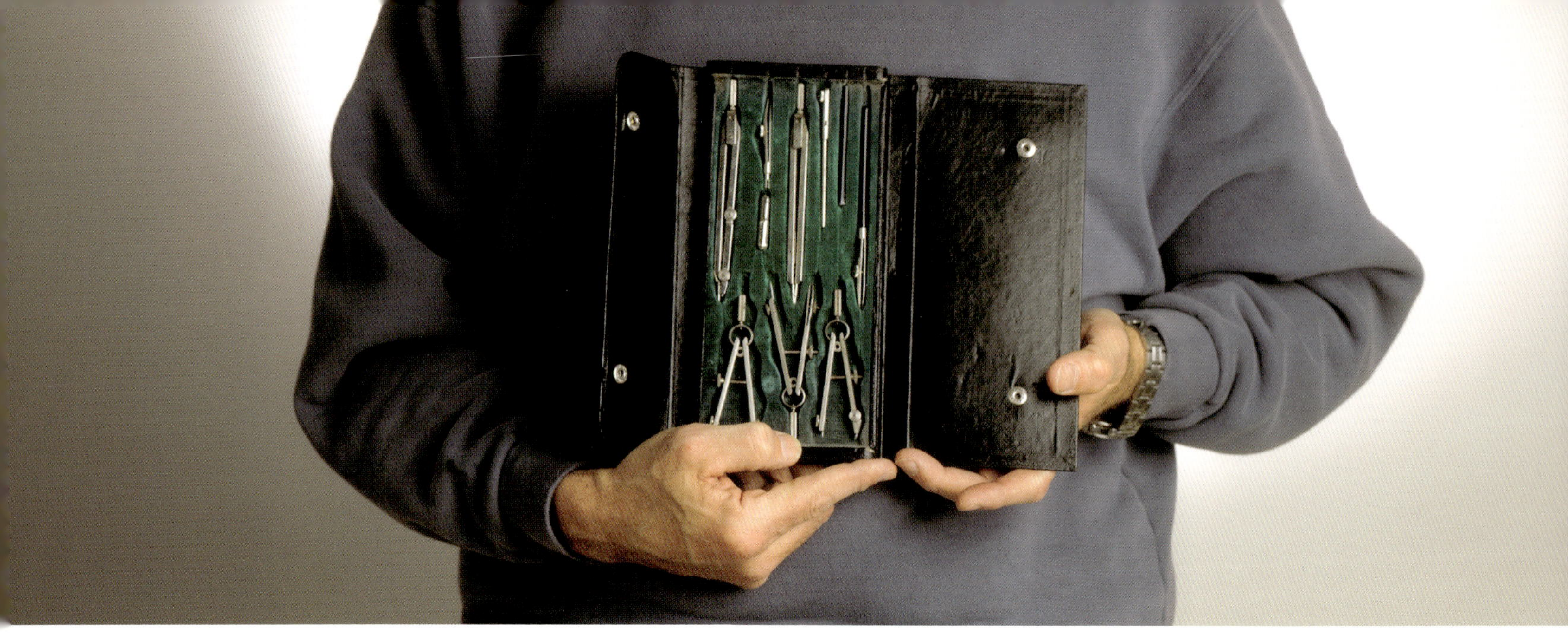

ABOUT ***PRECIOUS OBJECTS***

This project began when a friend (who happens to own a Rolleiflex which belonged to a photographer we both admired) asked me what was my most prized possession. I could not answer. In fact, having just prepared to move and dispose of what seemed to be a mountain of stuff, nothing I owned seemed that important anymore.

Are objects important? Ours' is a consumer society, and we are told that our purchases drive our economy. I began to photograph friends in my studio with my 8x10 camera, asking each subject to hand-write a few sentences about their choice. The wooden camera helps mediate the power relationship between photographer and sitter, and the large camera allows me to cut out the object and enlarge it by itself.

The setup was designed to let us learn about the person through their story, their dress, their handwriting and their posture.

Originally, the plan was to compare these personal choices to consumer culture. Sneaking into department stores with my digital camera, I was a regular 007. The final work would consist of the portrait, the enlarged object, similar objects as they are displayed in stores and the written statements. Ultimately, this was abandoned. The stories were just too compelling.

At the opening of the annual Juried Membership Exhibition of the Houston Center for Photography (HCP), it occurred to me to arrange a precious object shoot there.

With a tremendous amount of help from staff and volunteers at the Center, including the use of a studio owned by two of their instructors, we did our first remote site. People affiliatied with HCP, friends of friends and even some responses from Craig's list participated. This was followed with sessions in Atlanta, Los Angeles, Manhasset, Hempstead, Columbus, and Beachwood. What had been friends, their family and friends now was a much wider and diverse population.

Most of the 175 people who participated in *Precious Objects* were strangers to me. Rarely did I know what they would bring to the shoot or how they would dress. If they asked, I discouraged easily replaceable things. Only living things were not allowed as objects. Generally, I did not know anything about the participants or their object until after the photography was done and they had written their statement. This is not classical portraiture. To the extent possible, the subjects are telling their own stories.

This project began with a focus on my wanting to compare these things[what things?] to contemporary consumer objects. In the making, the project evolved substantially. The overall collection is not about what I think or is it even about the objects. It looks at the personal search each subject makes through the material in their lives to discover the stories that link the objects to who they are today. In some cases, participants knew what they wanted instantly. Some people never were able get there.

There are many ways to view these studies. Sometimes it is the story, and the photograph is merely an illustration. Often, appearance counts. Curiously, the handwriting often looks like the photograph.

My view returns as I select subjects to appear in this book or in an exhibition. It is impossible to ignore my own history or the things I love and respect.

I am humbled by the stories of the 170 people in this project... Loli's letters written by the mother she never knew, Trevis' inmate card from 25 years ago and his current library card, and Grace's lovely little stuffed dog who survived her scarlet fever... all represent the subjects' courage and generosity in coming forward with their stories. While all three are challenges I never faced, they give life and perspective to the one's that I have. As time passes, another level of meaning emerges. I knew when he appeared with his inmate card that Trevis would be part of this project.

Now, much later, it occurs to me that his question "Who are you?" is directed at me.

Am I a photographer, an artist, a storyteller...? These people are speaking. I am taken with their humanity.

Chuck Mintz
May 15, 2012

I love this wildcat because he's fierce!
Inside I have a streak of wildcat,
and he protects me.

I always wear a red hat because
I'm short, and people can't find me.
This way, my husband could always
find me in a crowd, & I'd never be
lost.

Muriel W. Reichen

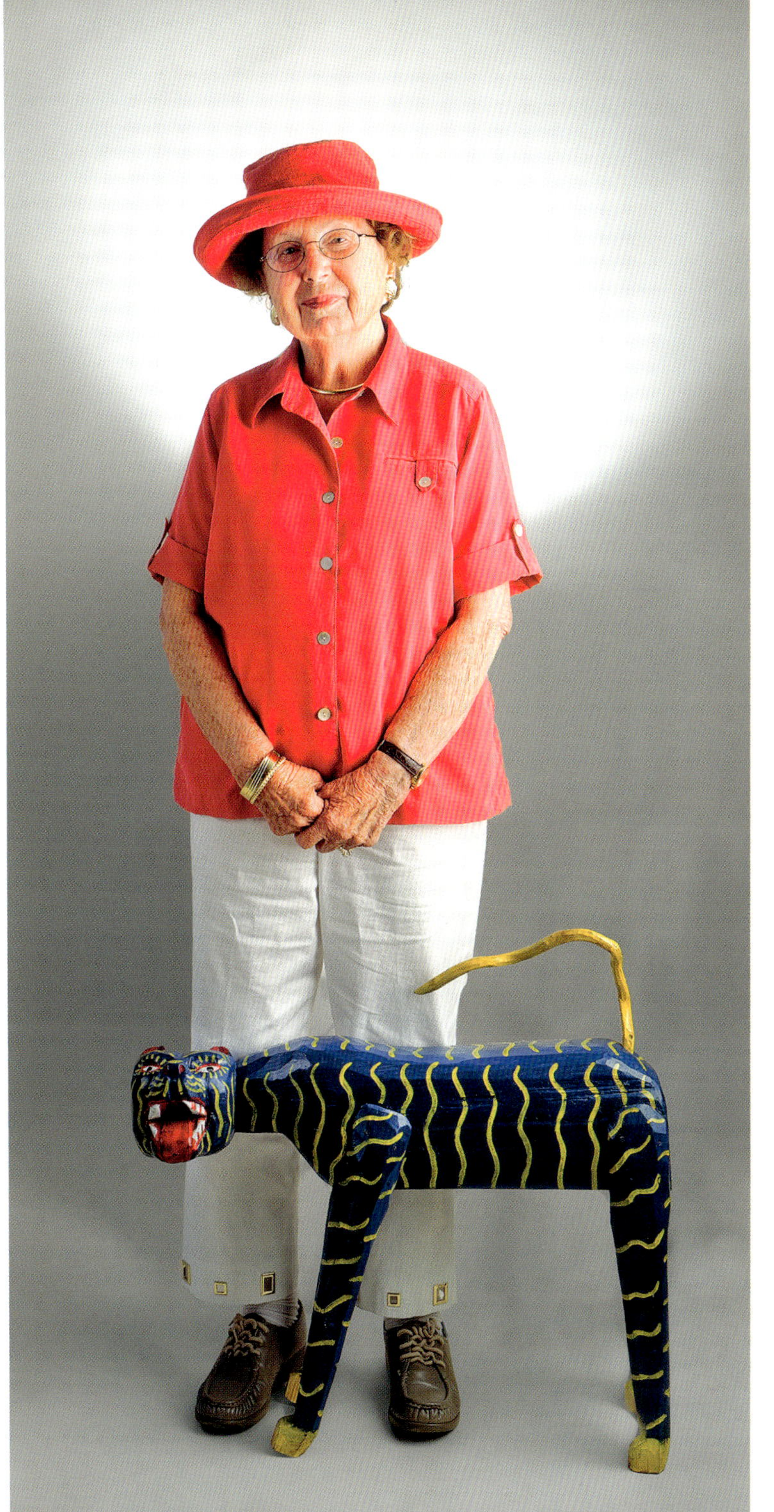

MURIEL

My earliest, vivid memory was when I was about 3½ years old. My family was at a summer party. In the midst of all this happy activity, my grandfather was taken away on a stretcher. He made the ambulance drivers stop by me as he was taken away. With difficulty, he reached into his pocket & gave me a dime, saying he was Santa Claus.

He died that day.

JOHN

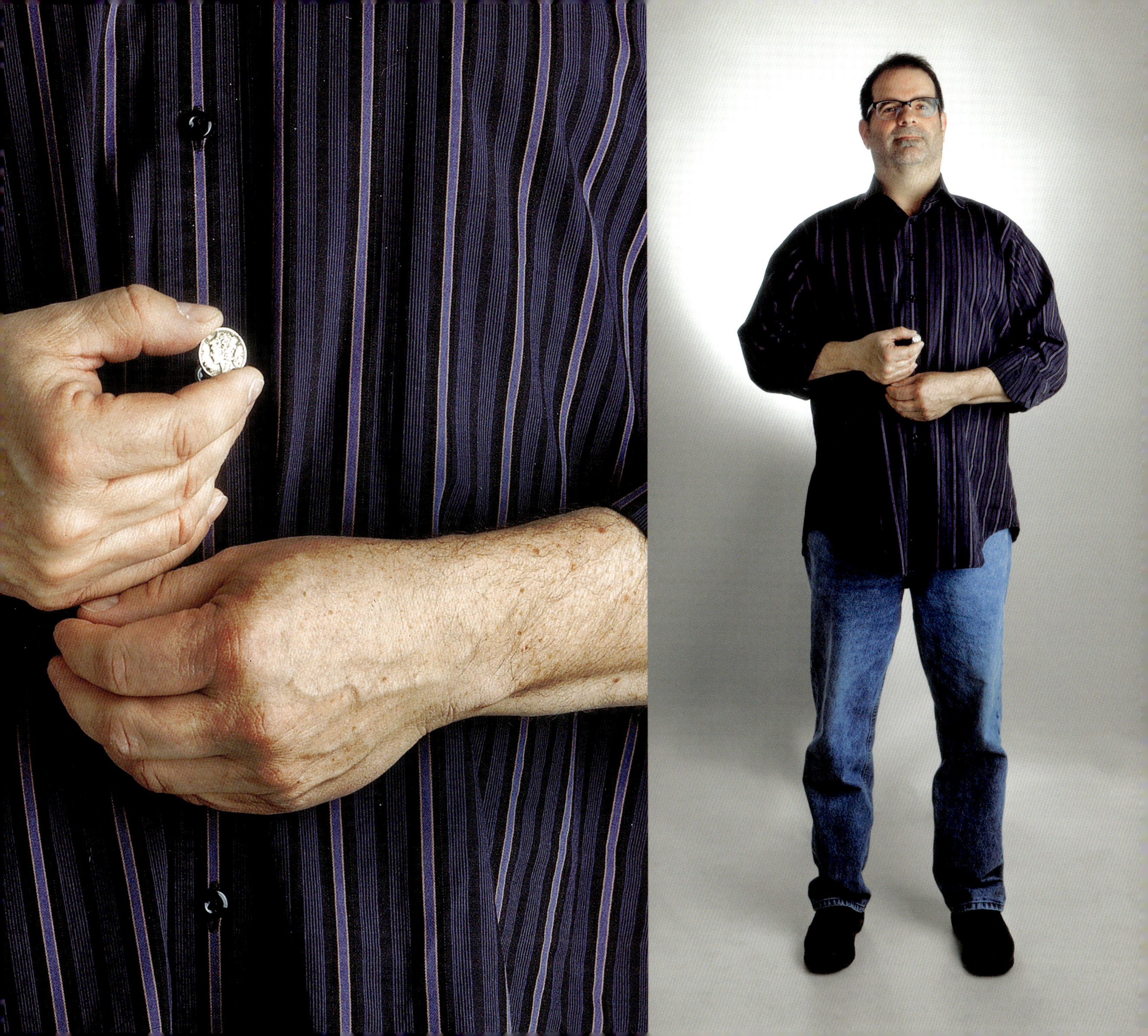

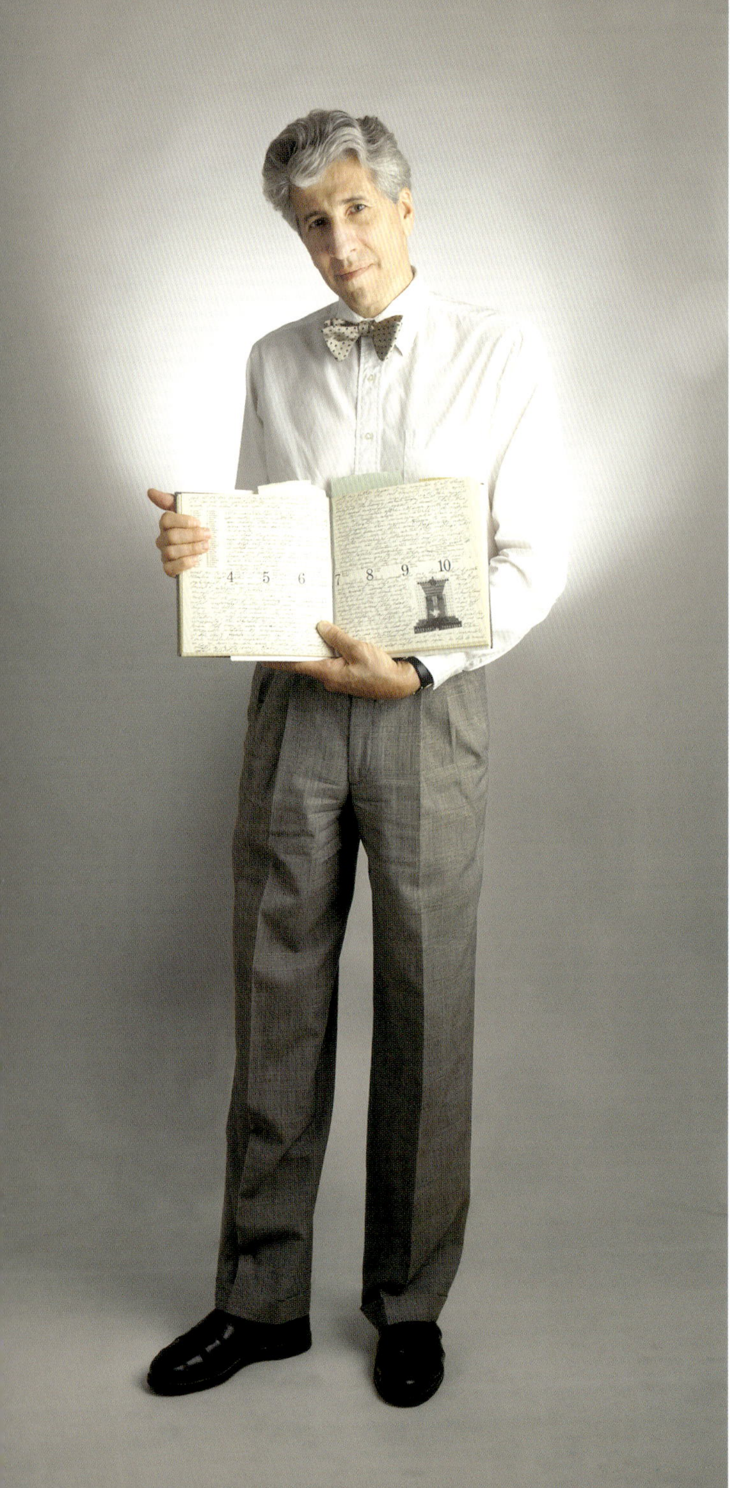

shortly
after the birth
of our first child
I bought a day
book to document as
a journal who we
were and all the
important events
that would transpire
through that early
time together. My
conceit and pride
at the time however
mandated that it
be "designed" and
in someway artistically
special so it
has a signed
original artwork
inside so our
son would someday
know that "all
that" mattered
to me.

ALBERT

I do think it is remarkable that I have held onto my very first camera, given to me by my parents to take on a 5th grade field trip on the Circle Line Ferry around the Statue of Liberty. I also have the first pictures I took on the trip — tugboats from a distance. Still — looking for the mundane and the majestic in the living landscape! The camera has a wonderful Sinclair dinosaur sticker on the back, vintage 1957.

GARIE

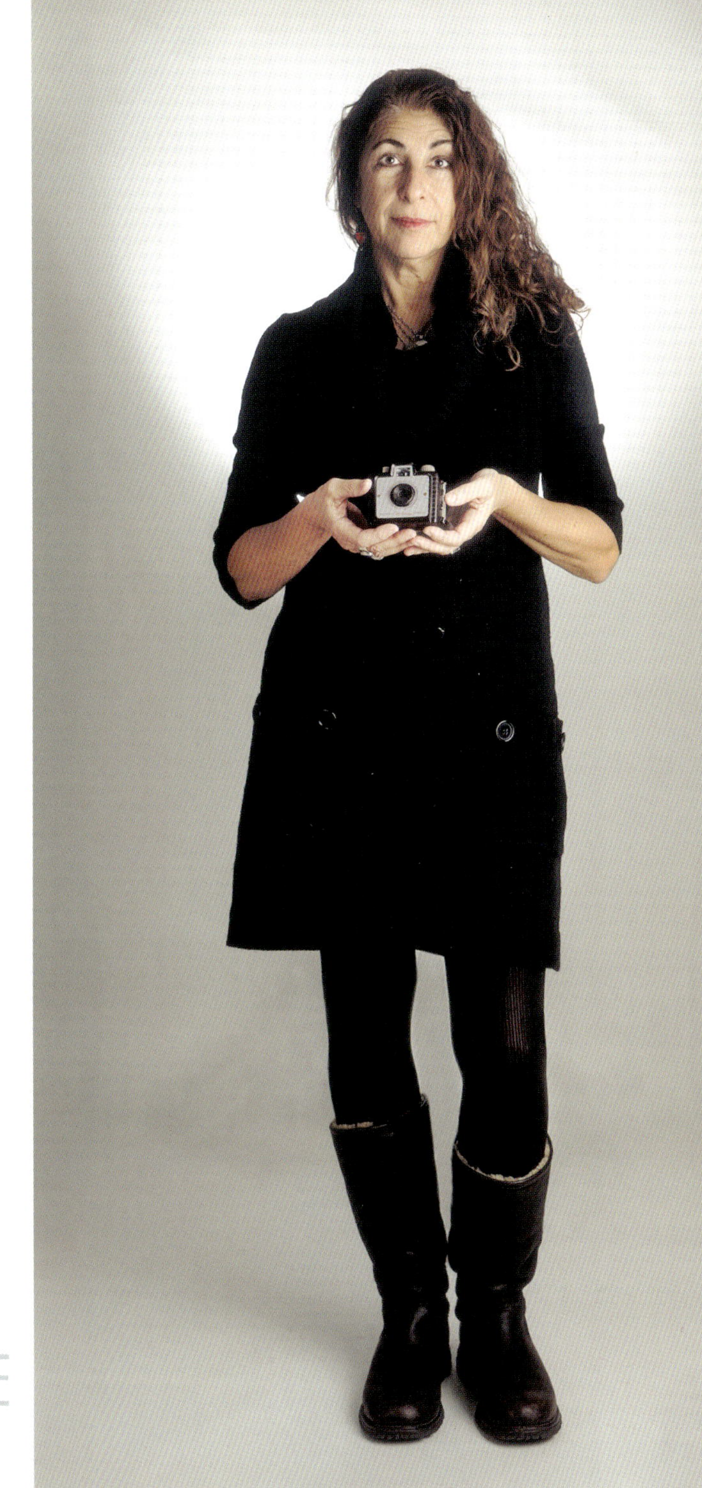

GANESHA !

My most precious object. I Got this at the age of
never Parted with it.
7, Have had it ever since. Have taken it to
school, college and is now with me here after
24 years in Cleveland, OH.

DEEPA VEDAVYAS
8/21/2010

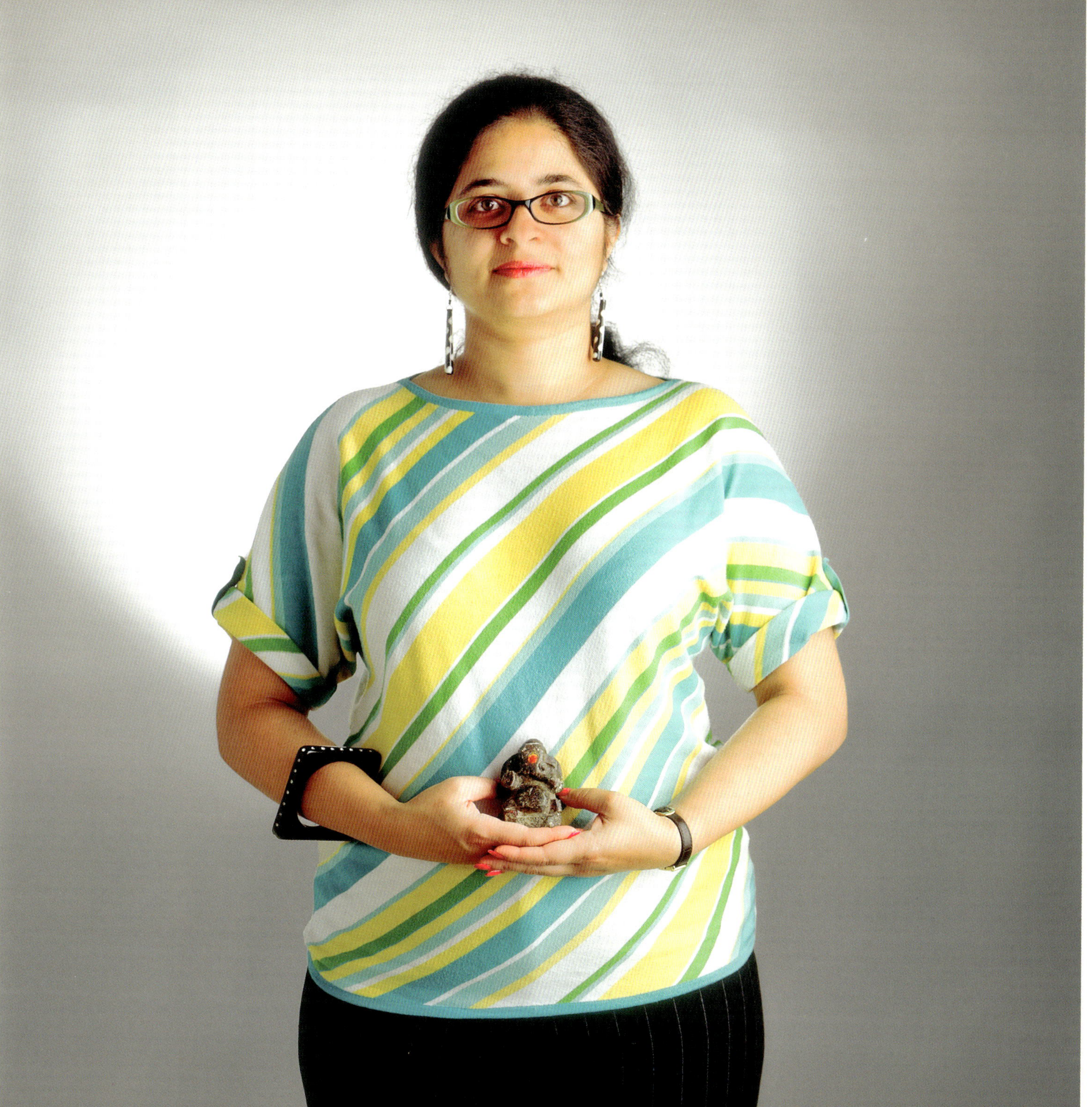

My I.D.

I Chose My I.D. to Allow People to See Me!
i Want them to Know me.
to feel me!
To help heal me
rebuild me.
Who am i? photo 1-2 or three?
Am i locked up or free?
A Stick or a tree?
it's My I.D
but which is me?
inmate?
Teacher?
Preacher?
A Doctor?
A lawyer?
Can you tell from the Cards i am holding in my hands?
Does it Depend?
And if you Knew would it Stop your World in its Spin.
Would it Keep you from Shaking my hand!?
its my I.D.
Who are you

—Trevis Moore

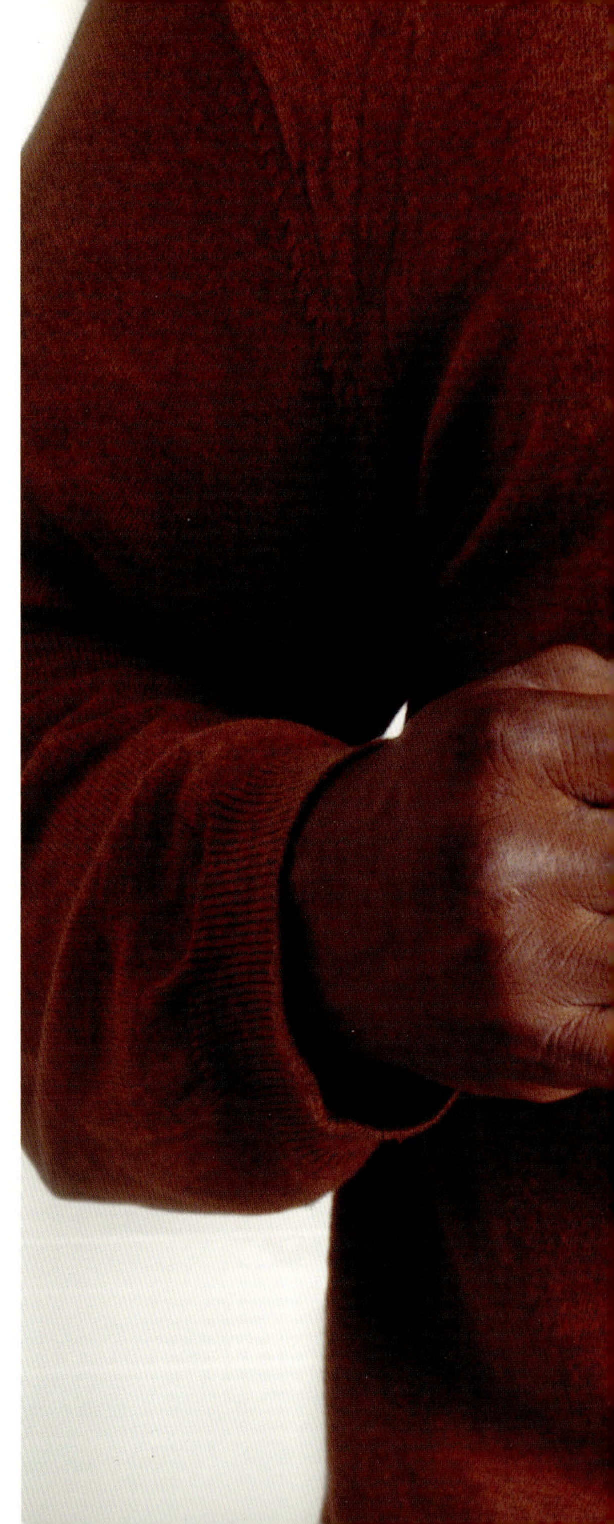

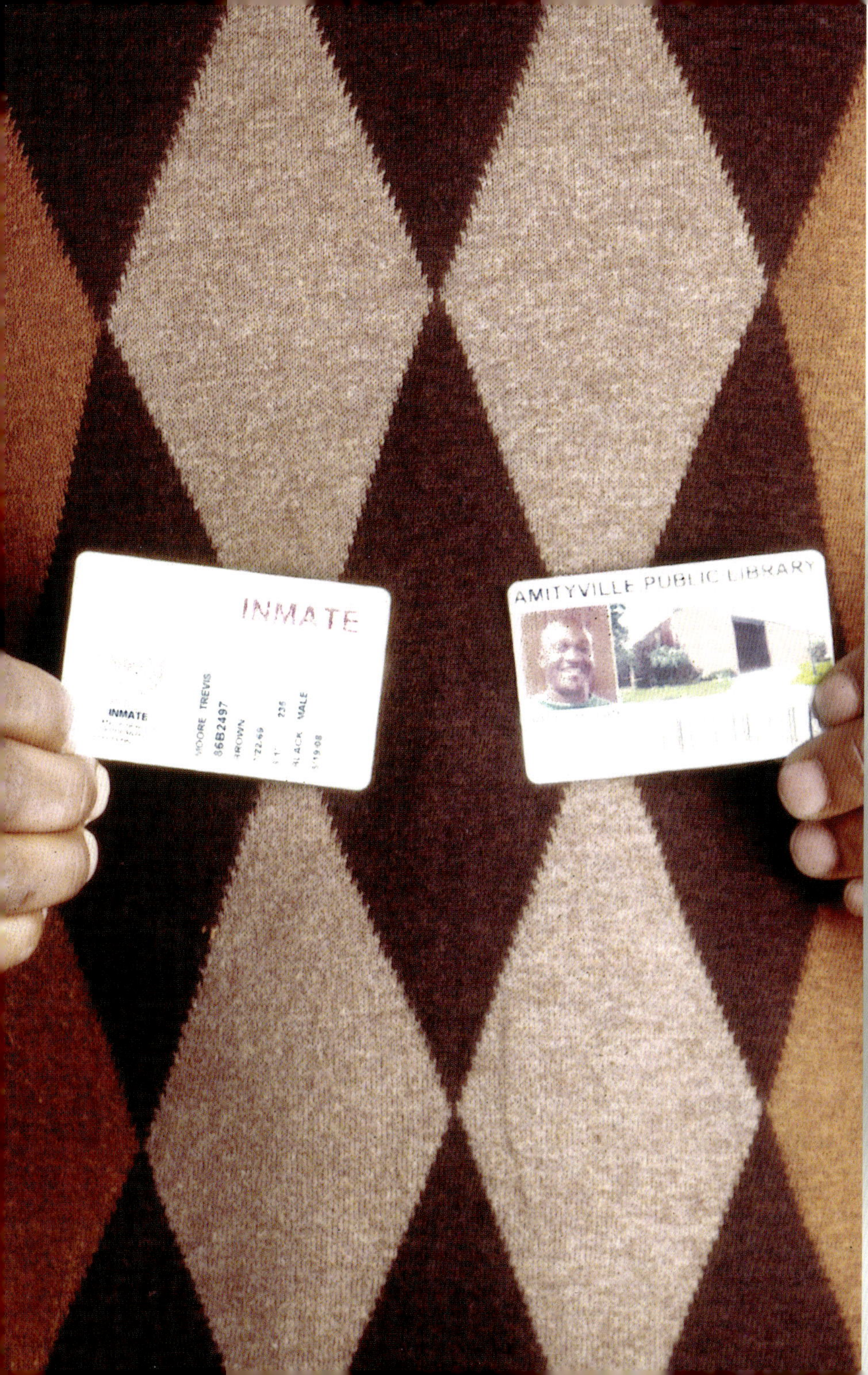

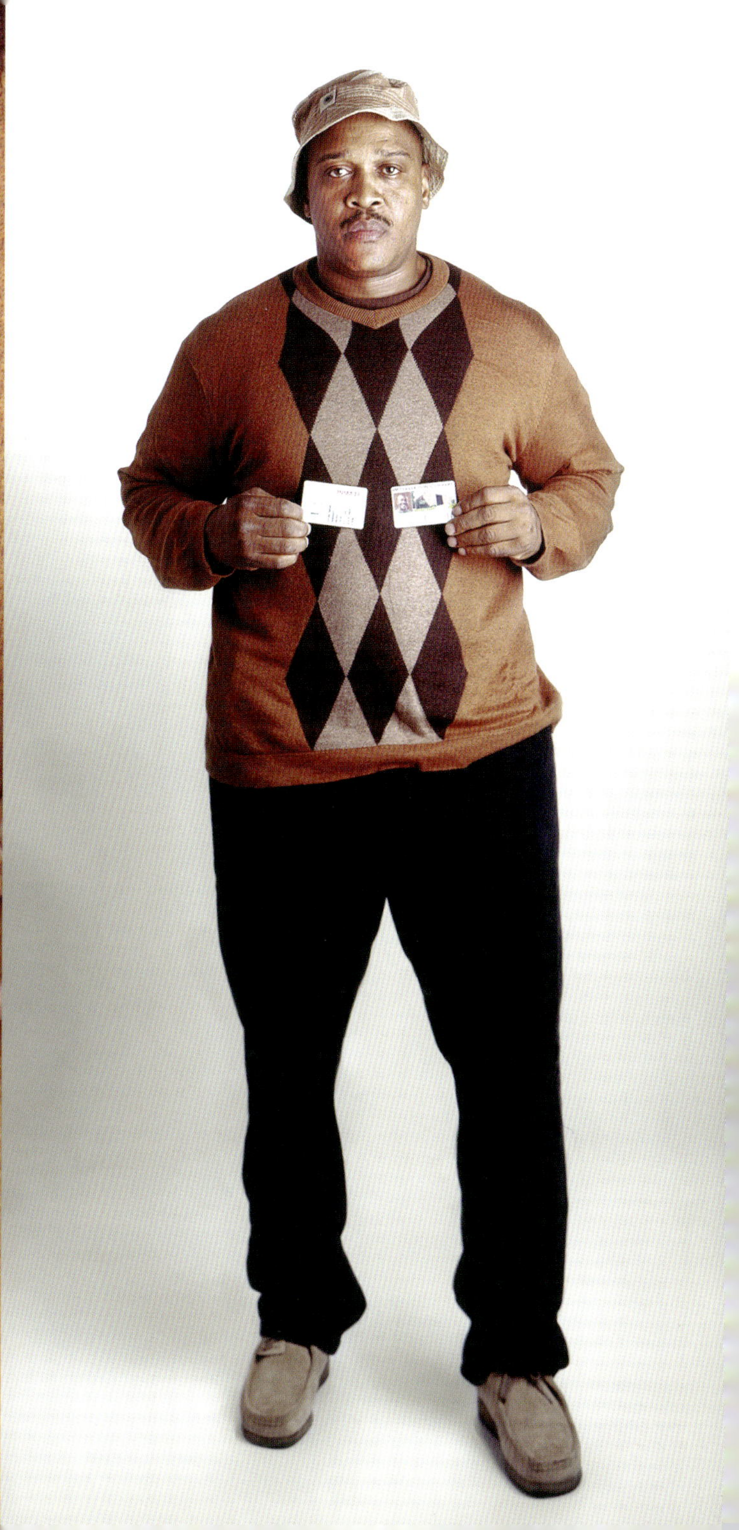

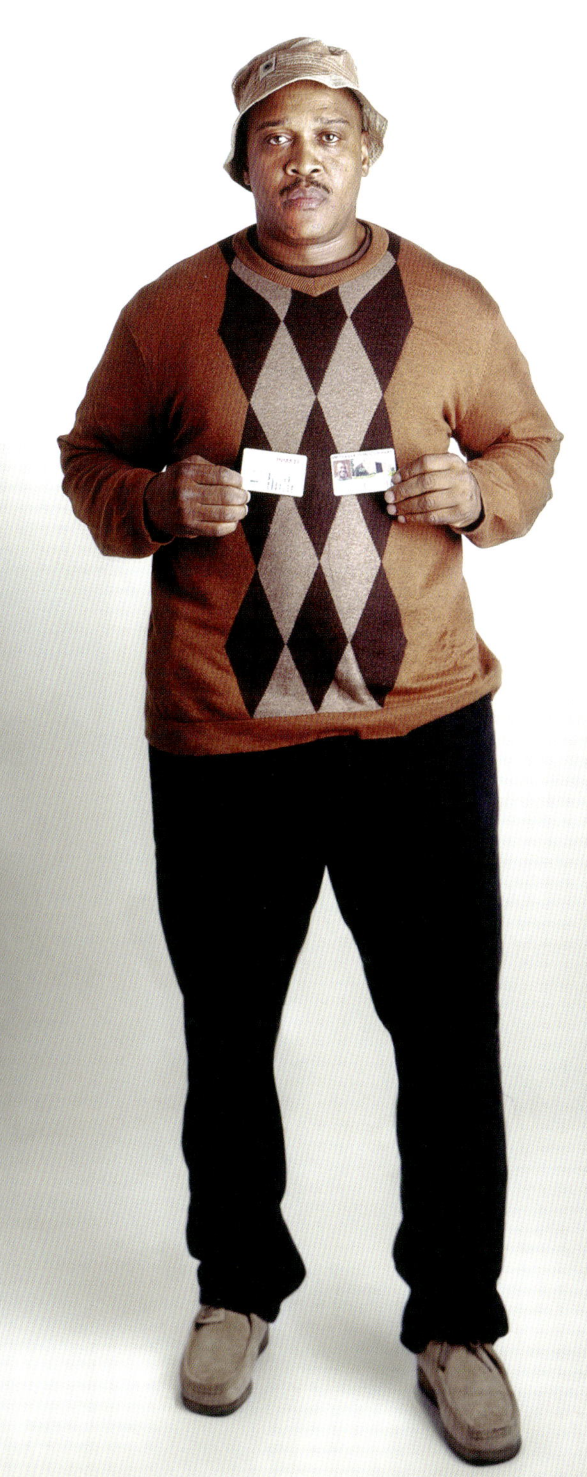

When i was 10 years old, I went to visit my arty aunt who lived in California, which was very exciting for someone who rarely traveled that far and who was happy making art projects every hour of the day. While we were together, we went to visit Buffy the Leather guy (an old California hippie), who custom-made this vest for me. It reminds me of the time I spent w/ my fave aunt who taught me it was ok to be creative and express myself however i needed to. Too bad the vest no longer fits.

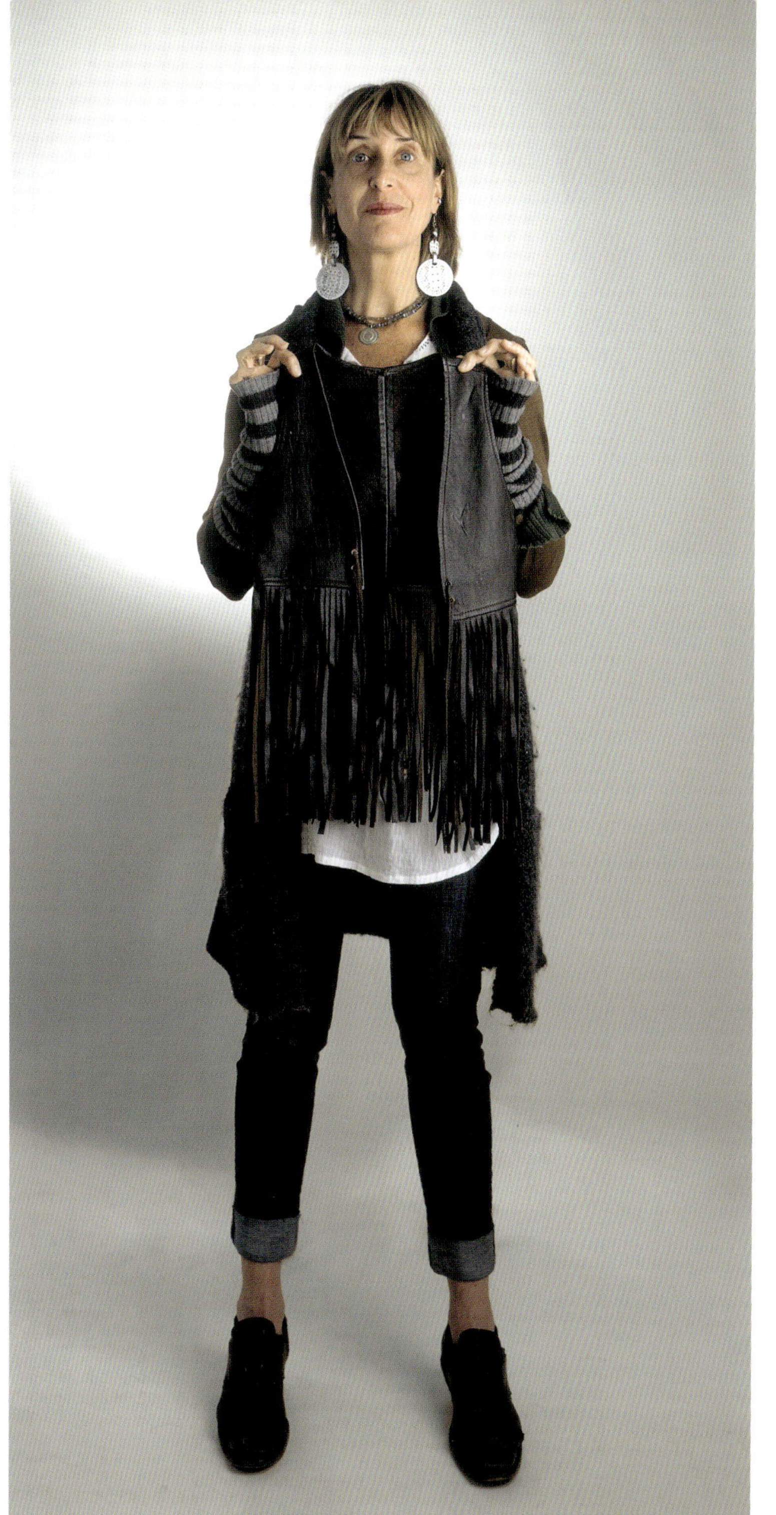

DEB

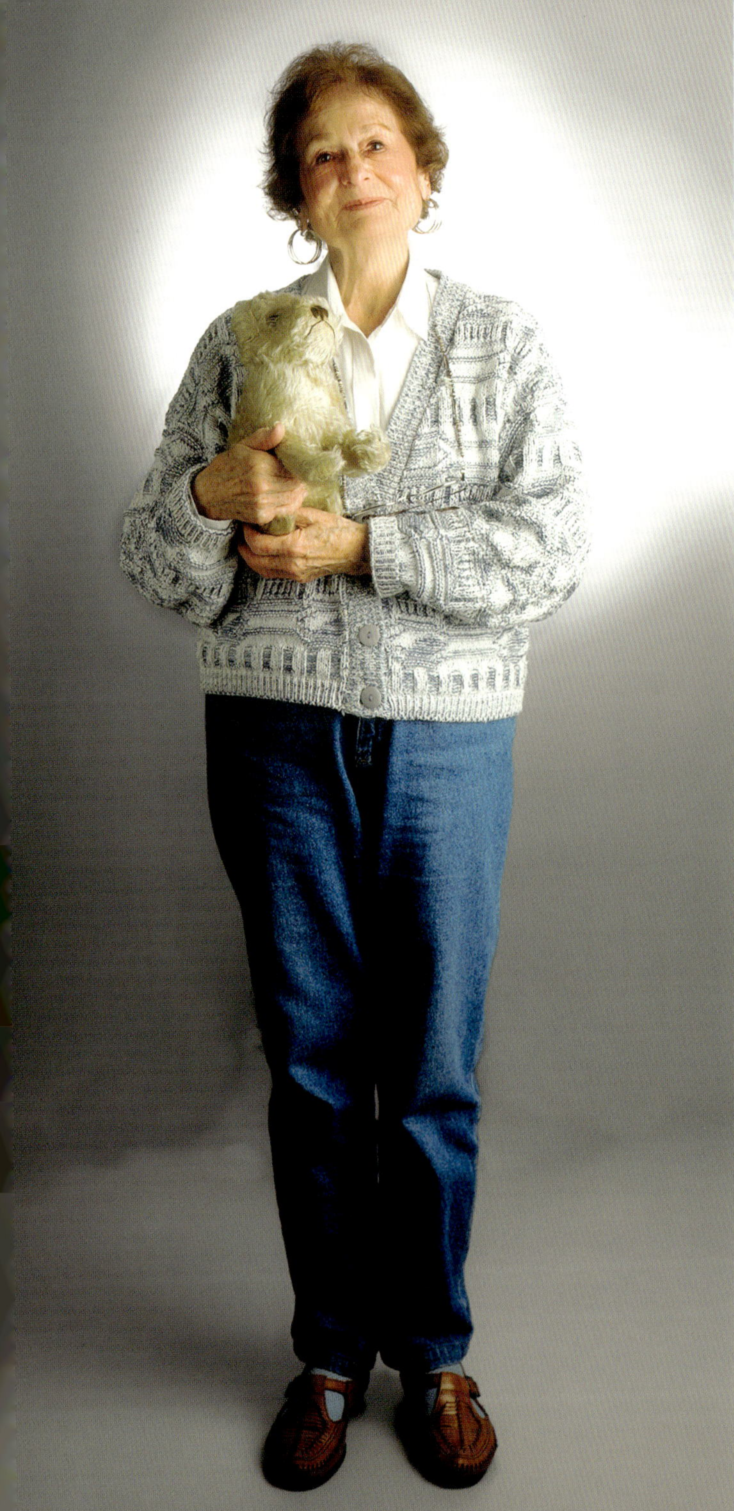

This is Trixie. She's been with me since my fourth birthday (I'm now 89). Unfortunately Trixie had to be sent to the dry cleaners after exposure to my childhood scarlet fever and came back not quite so plump and fuzzy as before, but she's still my beautiful and faithful Trixie.

Grace Ordin

GRACE

This Winnie-the-Pooh was given to me for Christmas when I was two years old. For many years, he was my nighttime companion and confidant. To me, his well-worn appearance indicates that he was/is loved very much.

KELLY

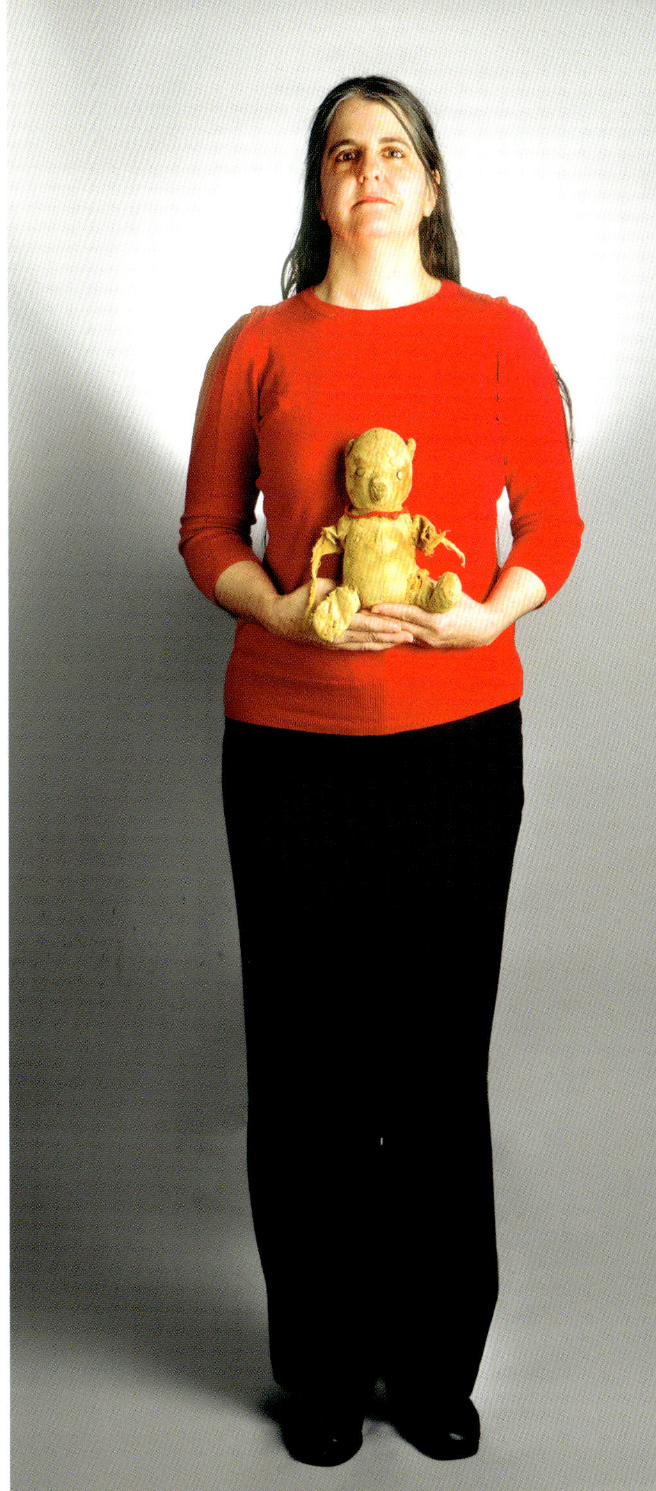

This pencil sharpener hung in our family kitchen for as long as I can remember. As a child I loved to play with it frequently using the shavings as 'pretend' tobacco which my buddies and I would roll into 'pretend' cigarettes and feel so "cool."

Recently my mother gave me this long after I had forgotten it. The sight of the sharpener, now hanging in my office, always prompts a smile and warm feelings of, probably, the happiest period of my life.

LANE

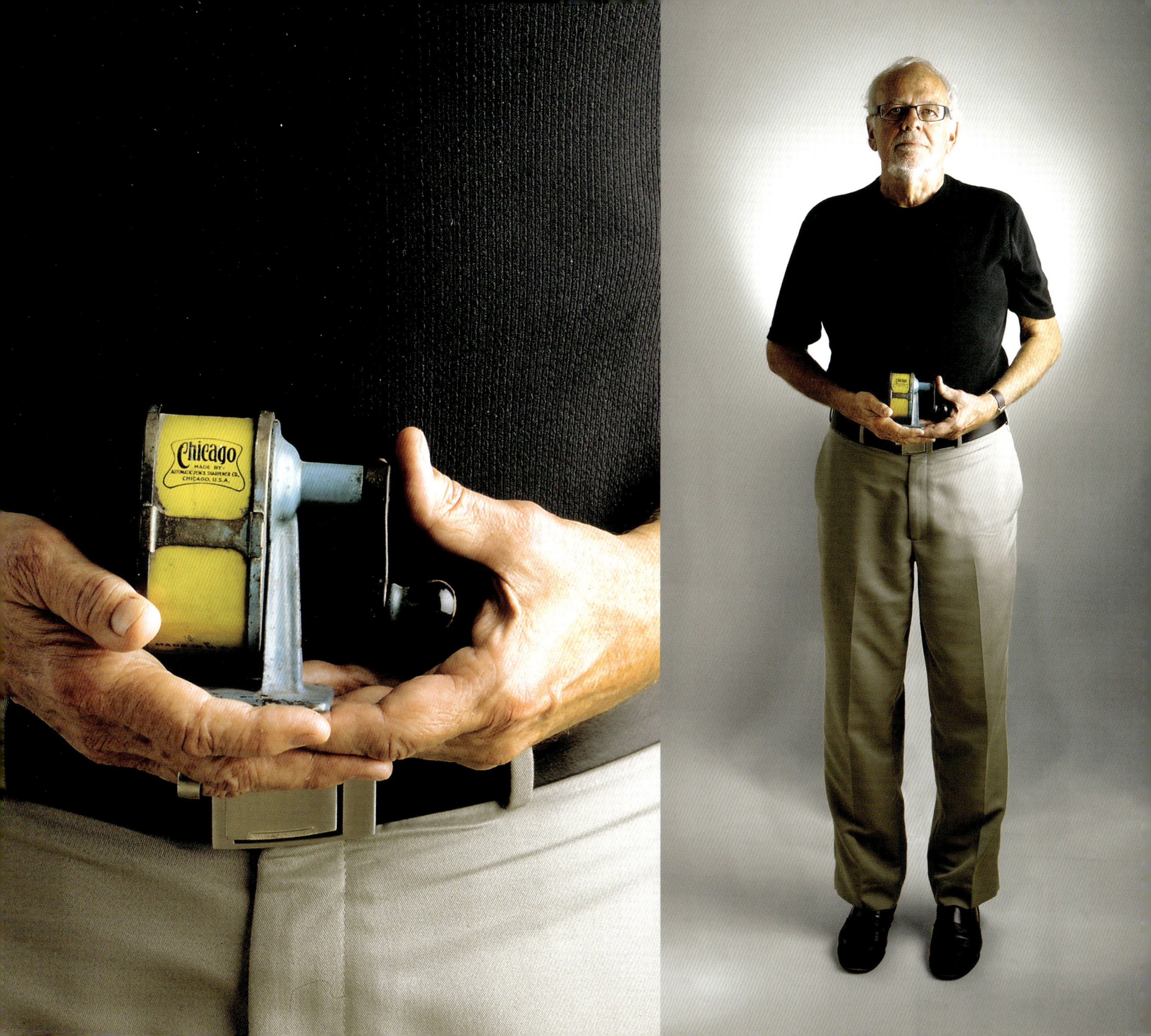
Chicago
MADE BY
AUTOMATIC PENCIL SHARPENER CO.
CHICAGO, U.S.A.

THE FRATERNAL 'SOUL' IS THE FIRST STEP TOWARD FRATERNITY IN MY SOCIAL FRATERNITY, KAPPA ALPHA PSI, AND AN OBJECT THAT I HAVE HELD AS 'PRECIOUS' FOR MORE THAN 40 YEARS.

FROM THE TIME THAT ONE PLEDGES, THE 'SOUL' TYPICALLY BONDS INDIVIDUALS THROUGH A PROCESS OF FORGING BROTHERHOOD, FIDELITY AND FRIENDSHIP, THROUGH GOOD TIMES AND BAD, IN PROFESSIONAL AND PERSONAL LIFETIMES OF EXPERIENCES.

IN THIS STAGE OF MY PROFESSIONAL CAREER AND FAMILY LIFE, THE 'SOUL' NOW SERVES AS A REMINDER TO ME OF A LIFETIME OF FRIENDSHIPS AND EXPERIENCES WITH SUCH LIFE-MOLDING FRATERNAL BROTHERS AND MENTORS AS CARL STOKES, MICHAEL WHITE, LOU STOKES AND MANY OTHERS WITH WHOM I BEGAN A BOND THROUGH KAPAA ALPHA PSI AND CONTINUES TO A NEXT GENERATION WITH MY SOON-TO-PLEDGE SON.

TERRY

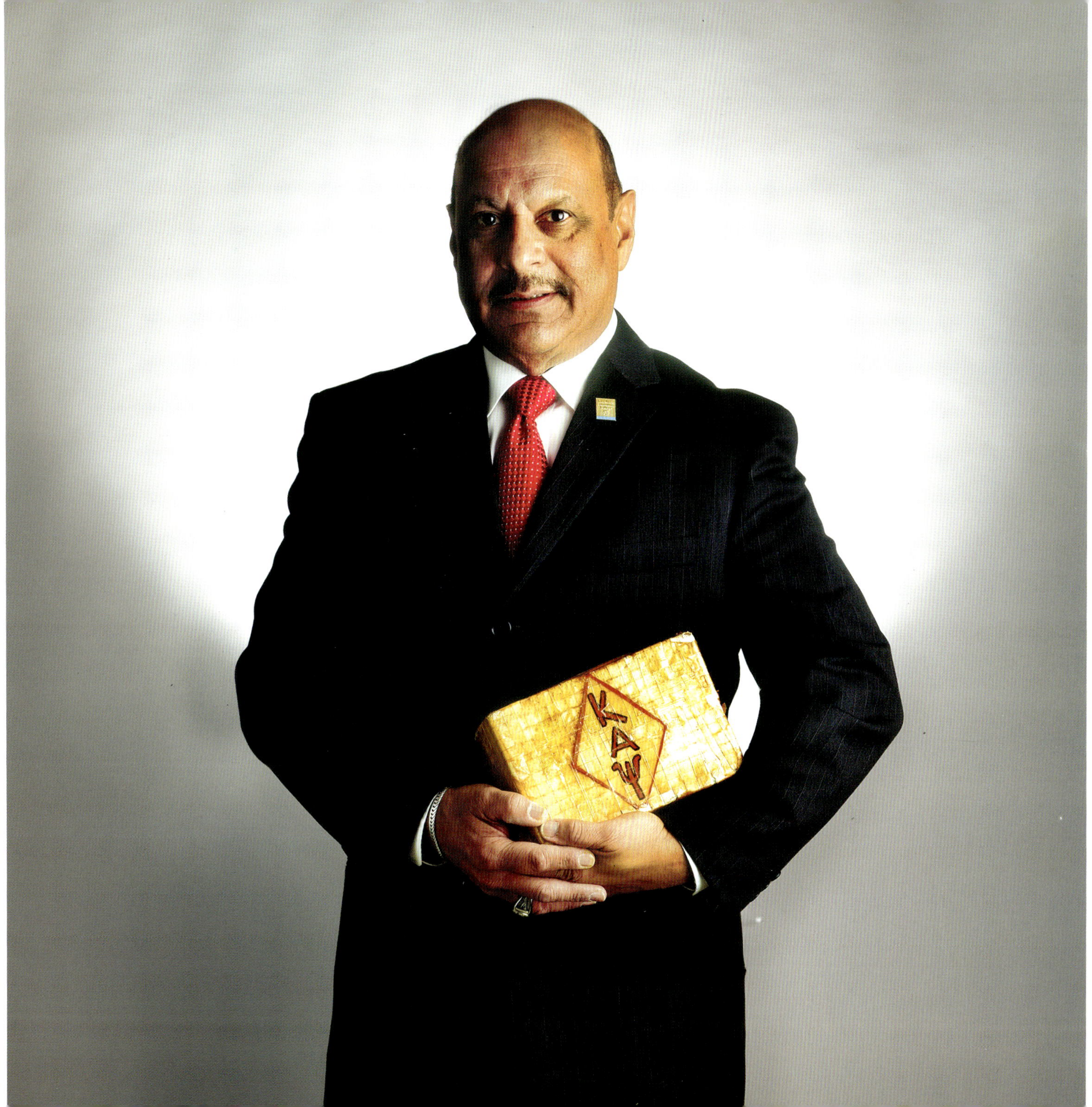
ΚΑΨ

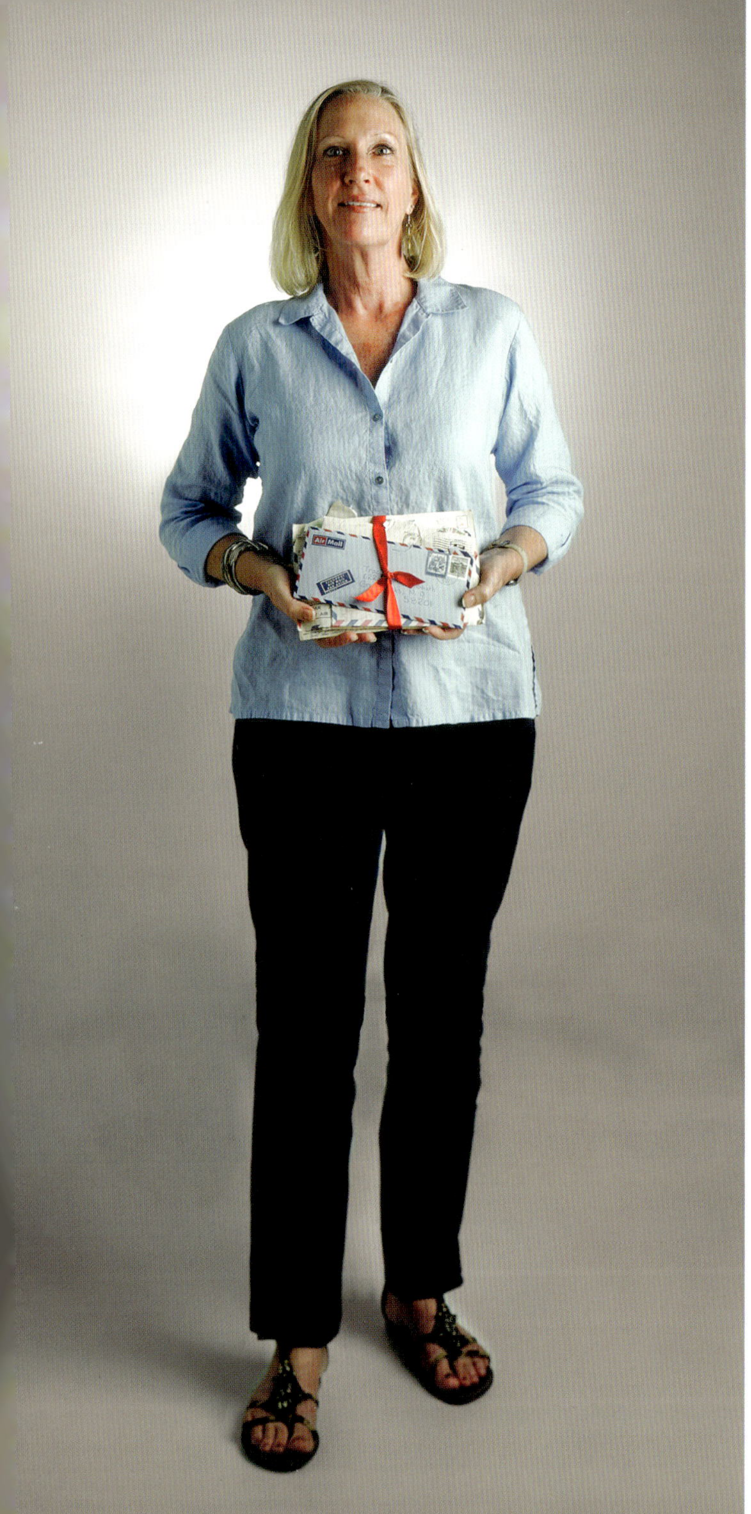

When I was eighteen, my family moved to Saudi Arabia leaving me in North Dakota. The last time I saw my mother was at the airport as I saw my family off. These are her last words to me.

XAVIA

This post card is precious to me because it was sent to me by my husband from the Fiji Island when my husband was serving in the army in world war two.

Sylvia Kramer

SYLVIA

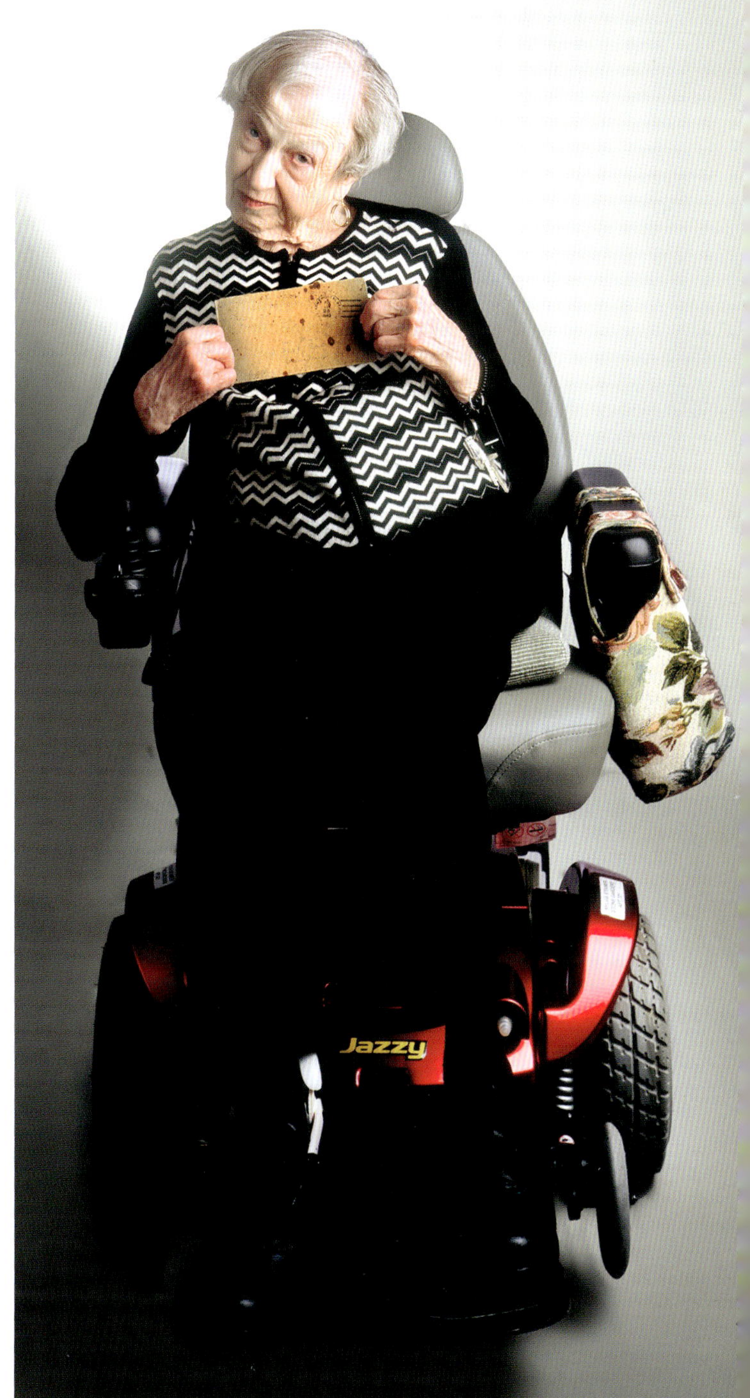

In the fall of 1967, the Veteran's hospital in Wade Park was full of injured Vietnam vets; my father was admitted with renal failure linked to his WWII tour of Duty in the South Pacific. While visiting him, I fell in love with a beautiful pajama doll I saw in the exchange window display.

He was critically ill at Christmas so we celebrated at the hospital, where he surprised me with the doll I stood and stared at so many times.

A few months later he died waiting for the experimental kidney transport program to begin. When I hold the doll, or see it perched on a closet shelf, I am transformed into a wide-eyed ten year old getting the gift of her dreams from her daddy, the last gift he would ever give me.

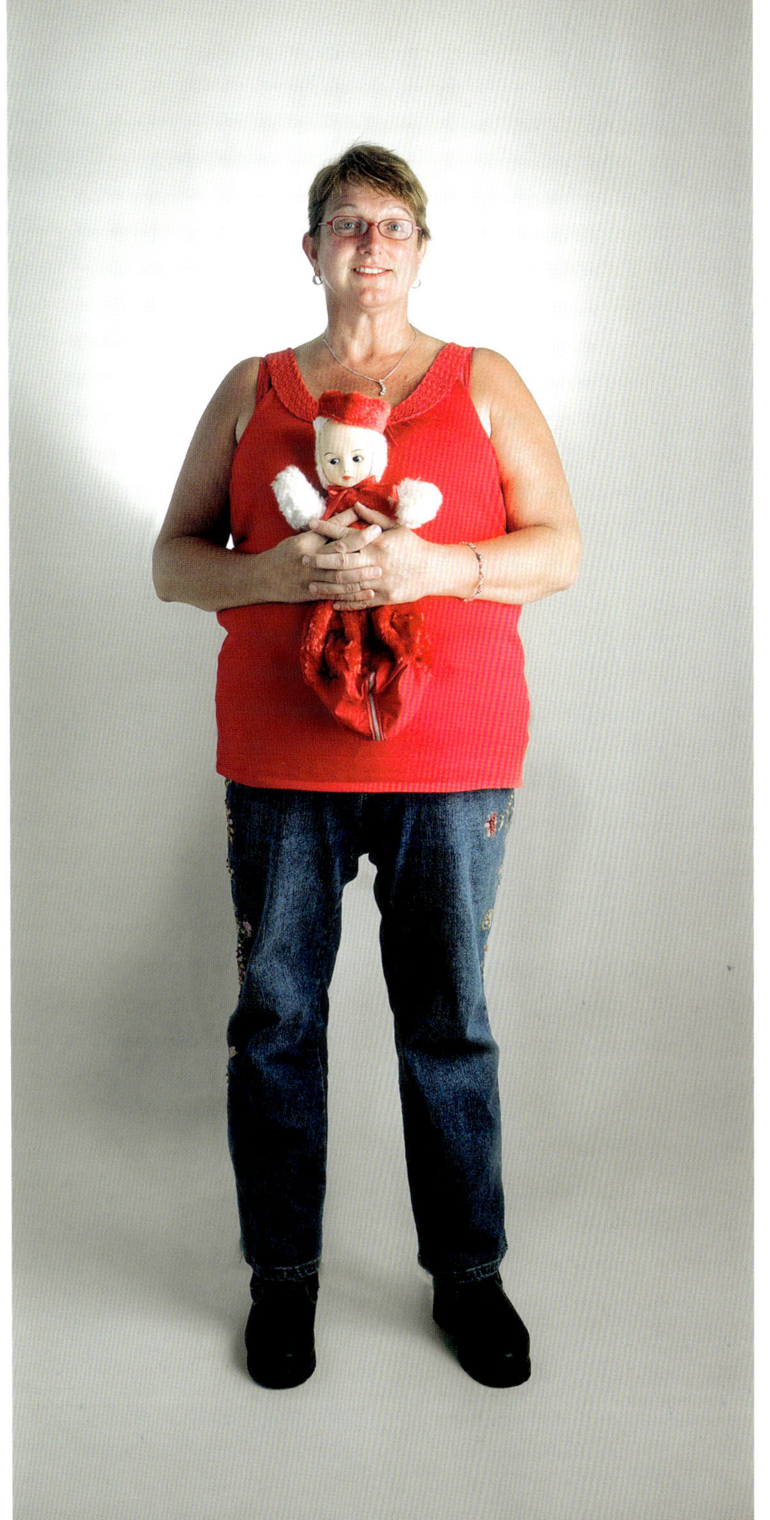

CHERYL

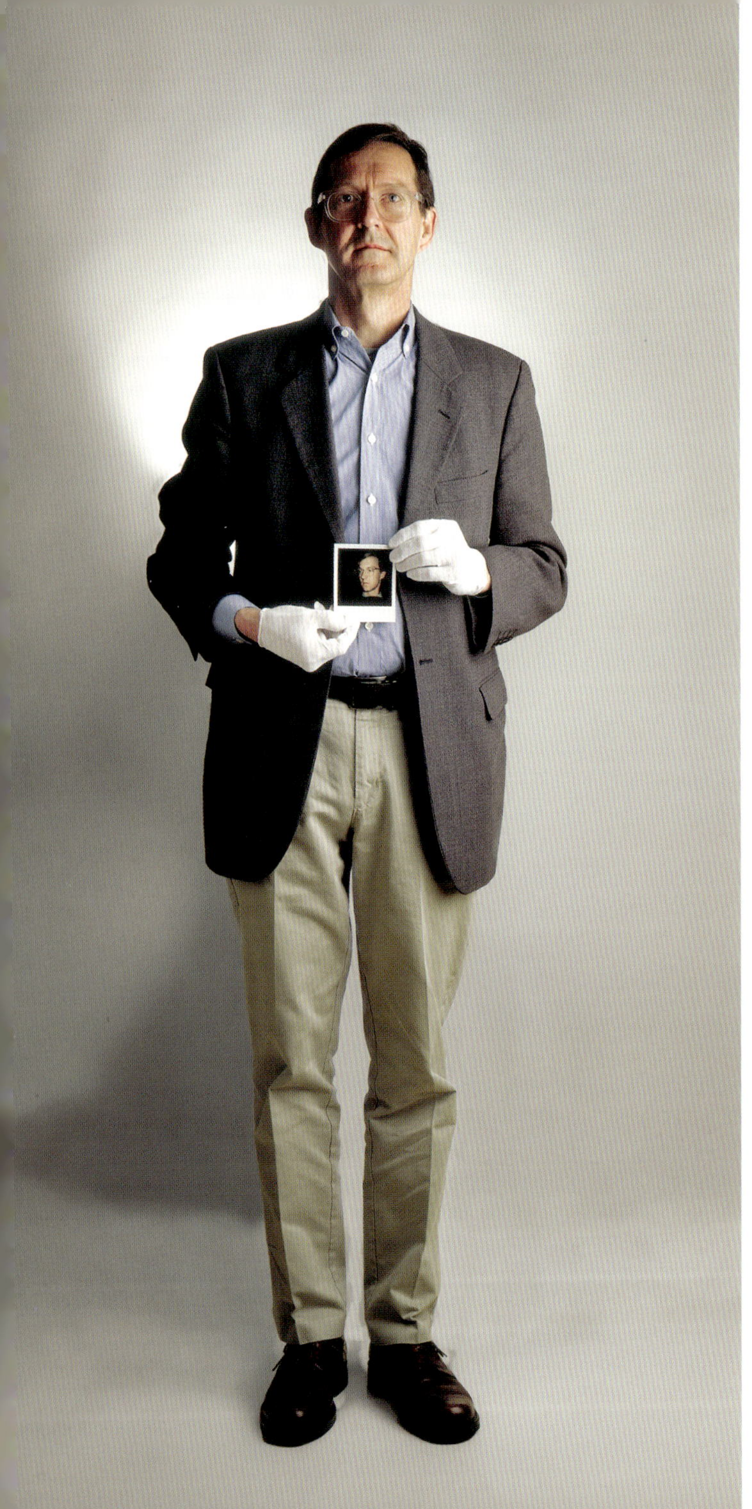

COLLECTING PHOTOGRAPHY IS MY GREATEST PASSION. THIS IS A PORTRAIT OF ME TAKEN BY WALKER EVANS IN 1974. I HAD COMPLETELY FORGOTTEN ABOUT THIS UNTIL MY BROTHER GOOGLED ME AND FOUND TWO LIKE THIS AT THE METROPOLITAN MUSEUM. I GUESS IT JUST DIDN'T SEEM THAT IMPORTANT TO ME AT THE TIME.

-FRED BIDWELL

FRED

I have no tattoos, but there are drawings that I carry in my memory. One of them is the 3,000 year-old White Horse, dug into an English hillside — a figure composed of shallow chalk-filled trenches. I have a piece of that chalk, and a stalk of wheat from a nearby field.

— Douglas Max Utter

DOUGLAS

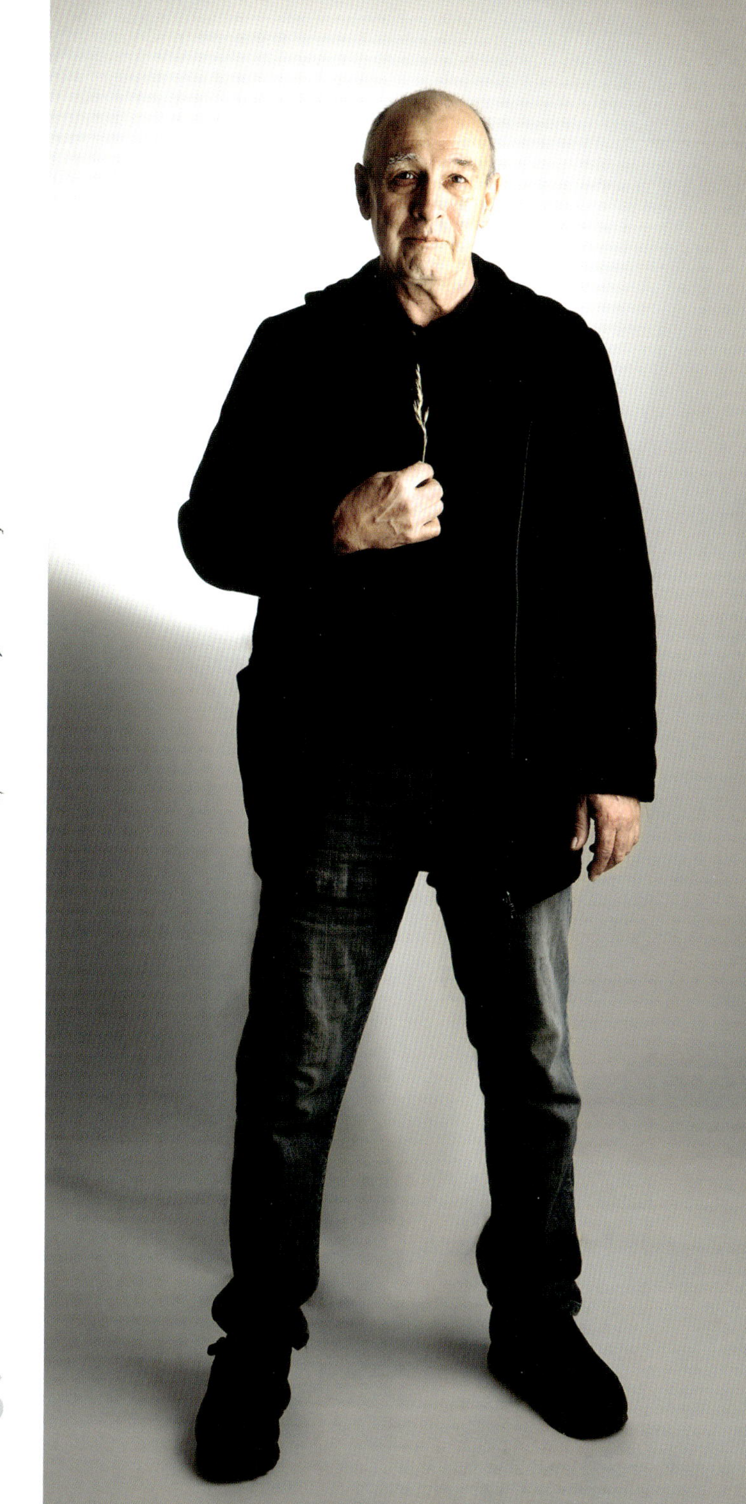

Loli Kantor

This is my mother's handwritten letter, dated April 21, 1946. My mother Lola Kantor, died in childbirth with me. This is the only handwritten ~~document~~ piece by my mother that I own.

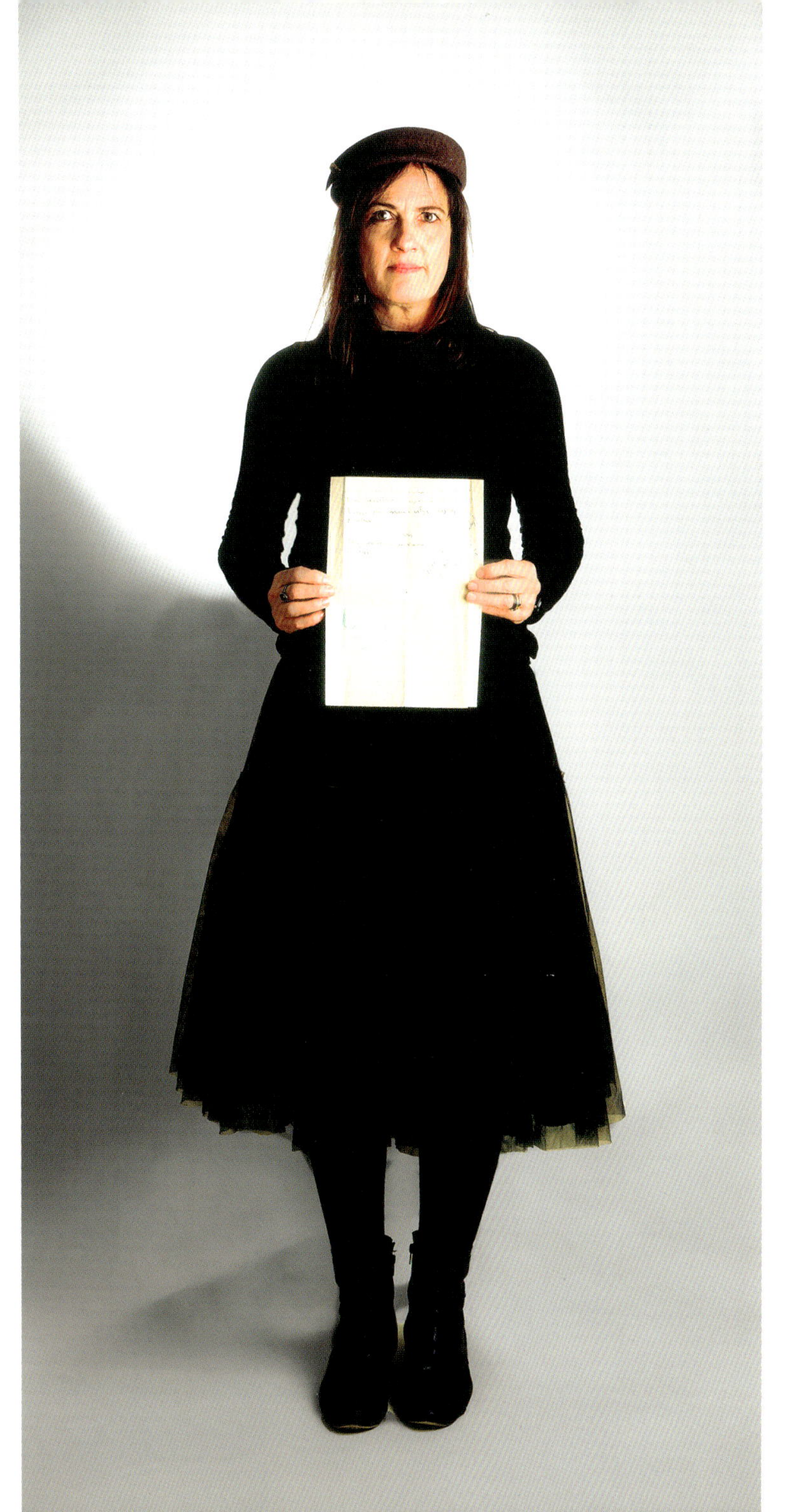

LOLI

My father was a very sharp dresser. When closing the house after his death, I found on the top shelf of a closet, carefully stored in boxes, two pairs of two-tone, winged-tip Allen Edmond shoes, one tan and white and the other black and white. When wearing them, I'm always reminded of him and his great sense of style.

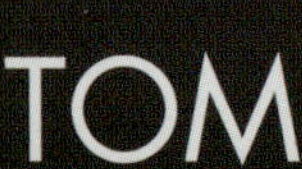

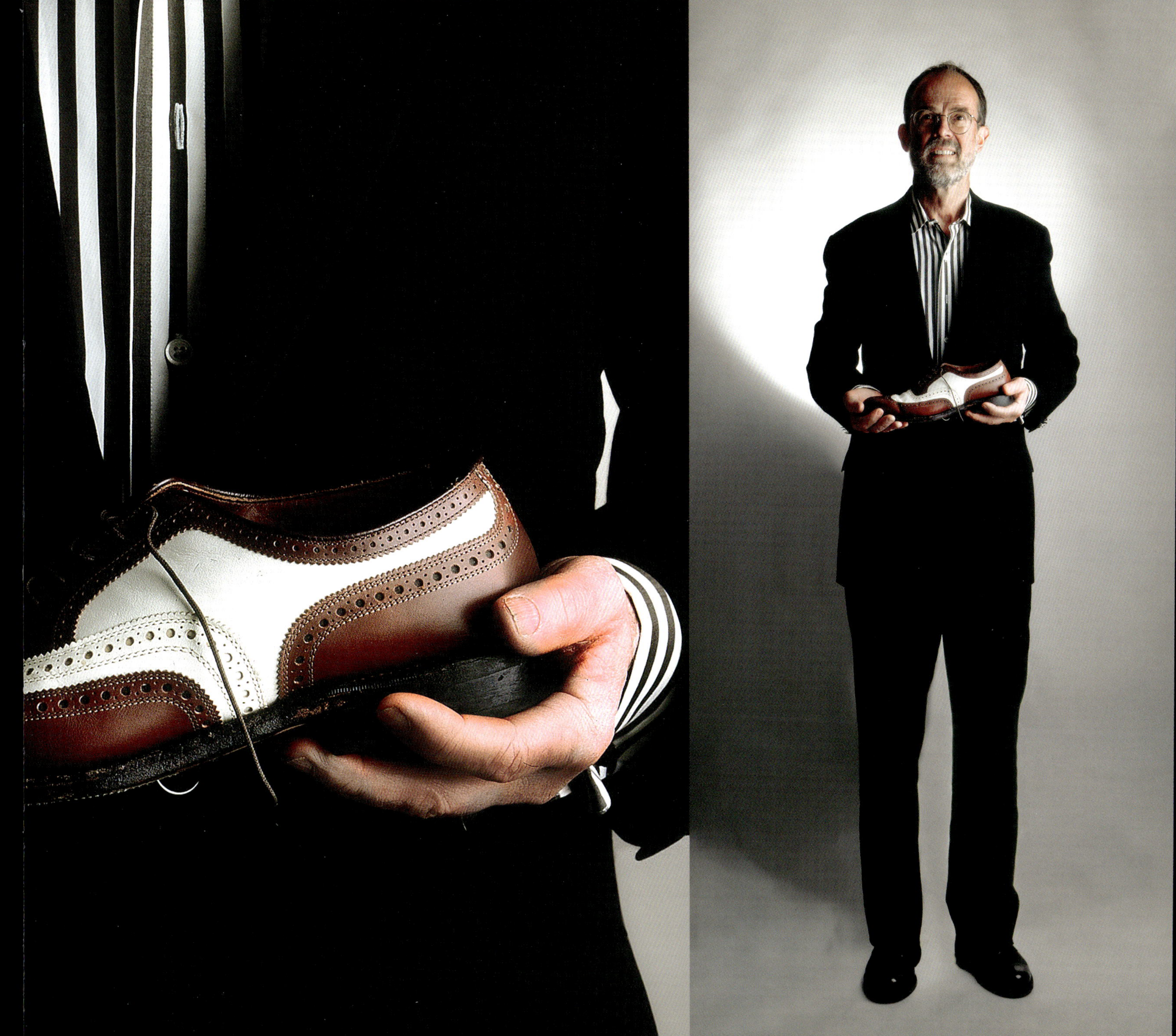

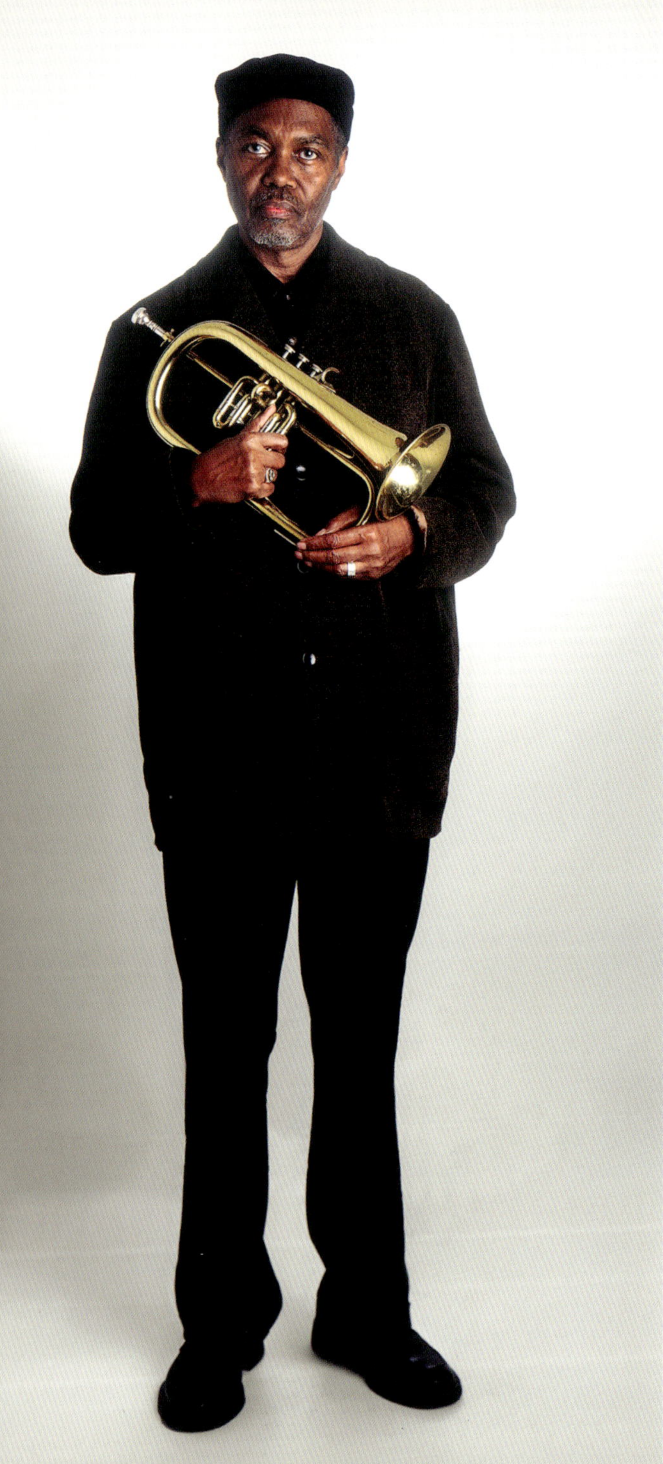

Norman "Naazir" Penson

Object: Flugelhorn

I discovered this Flugelhorn
at a Bronx music store while
purchasing materials for my students
in the early 1980s.
It was made in Paris and its
beautiful tone is one that
I will cherish and value forever

NAAZIR

This metronome, purchased in the 1960s, helped me, a Cleveland Orchestra musician, prepare to perform my "part" by indicating speed and accuracy of any given score.

MARTIN

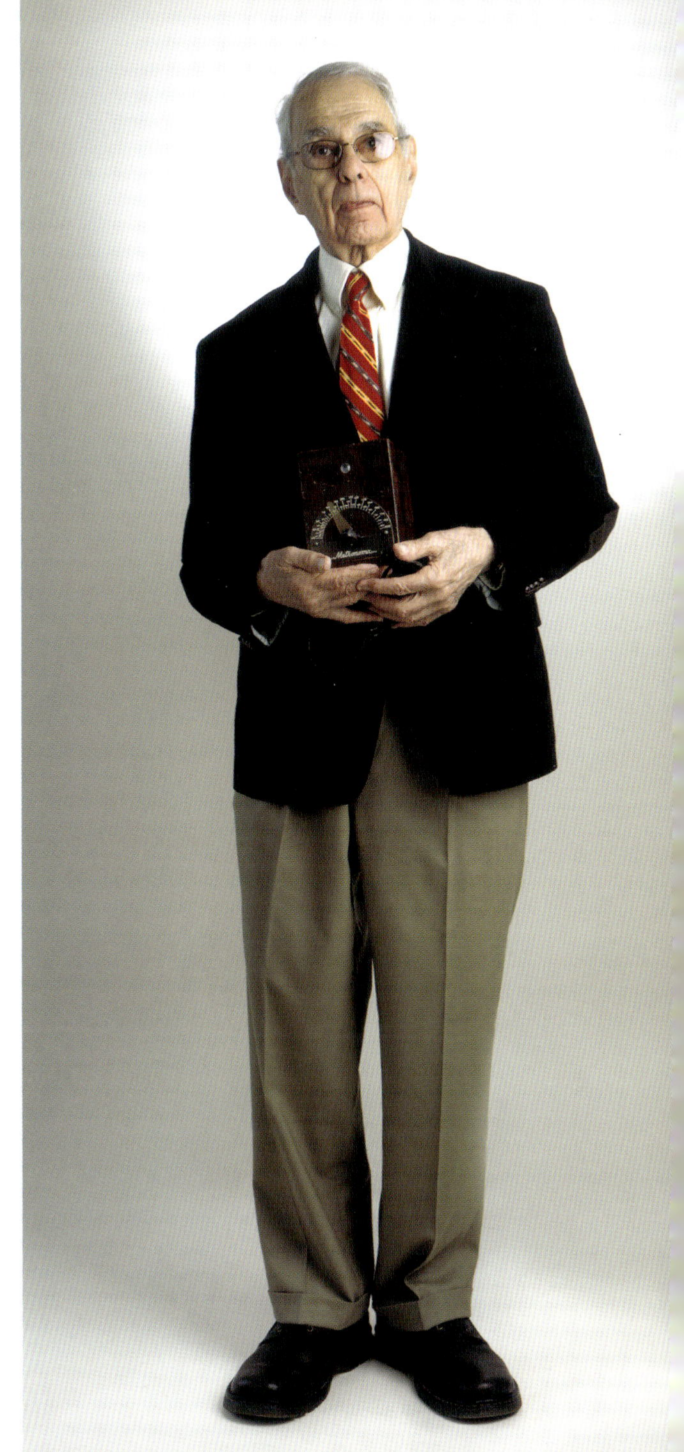

Roxane Lawrence

My Little Yellow Dress

I was adopted when I was 3 months old. On December 2, 1964, my parents arrived to pick me up, and I was dressed for the occasion in this little, yellow dress. My mother always told me that other babies come into the world naked, but I came in a little, yellow dress. What a lucky day - what a lucky dress!

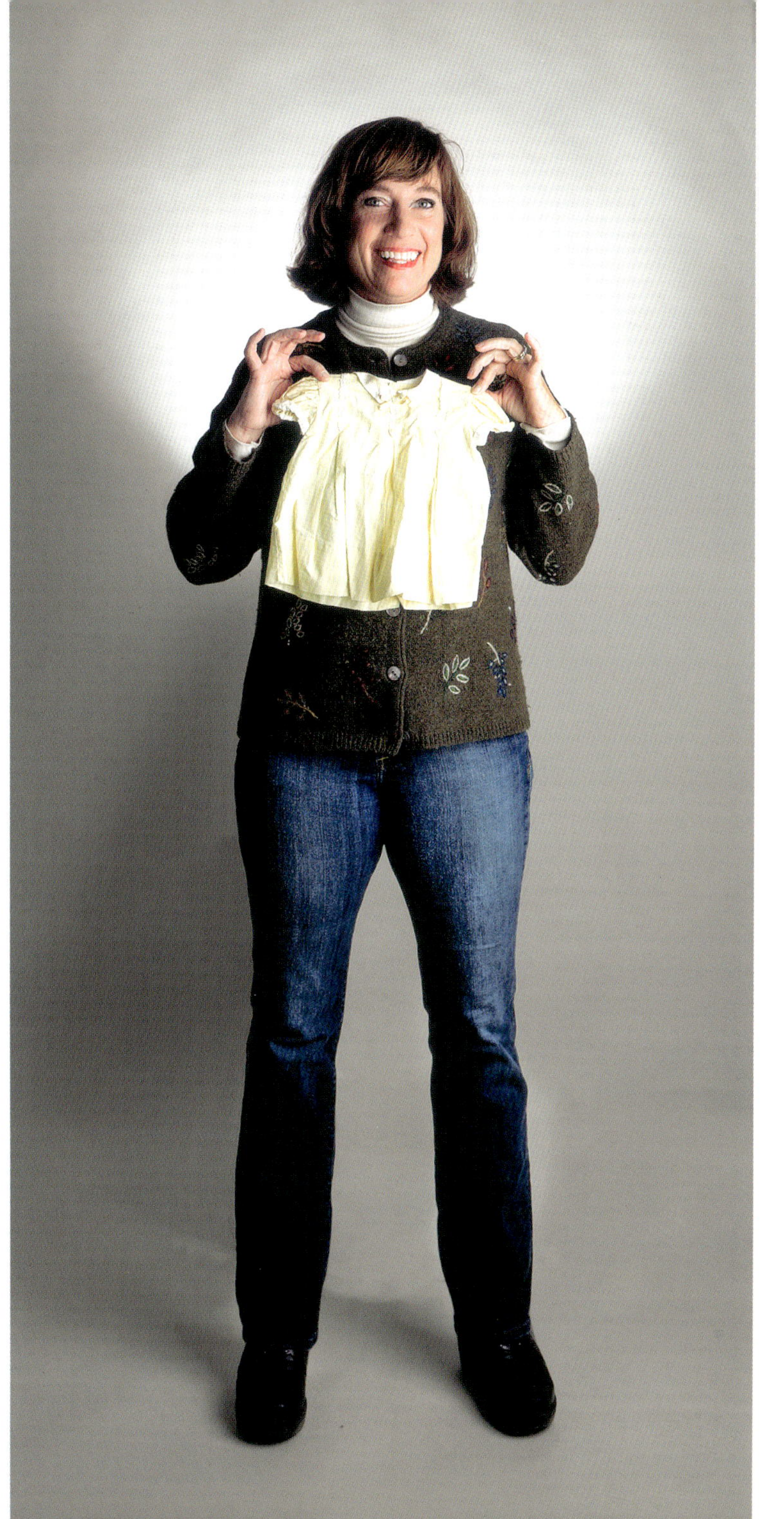

ROXANE

My dear friend Joey had a problem with drinking and drugs. He Called me in a panic to fly across the Country and bail him out after he had been arrested and put into Rehab. I flew to NY checked him out and tried to get him back into rehab in California.

He gave me this Rolex watch to show me what our friendship meant to him.

He died a few months later. I will always remember him - I recently learned he had bought it on time, and it had never been paid for.

GARY

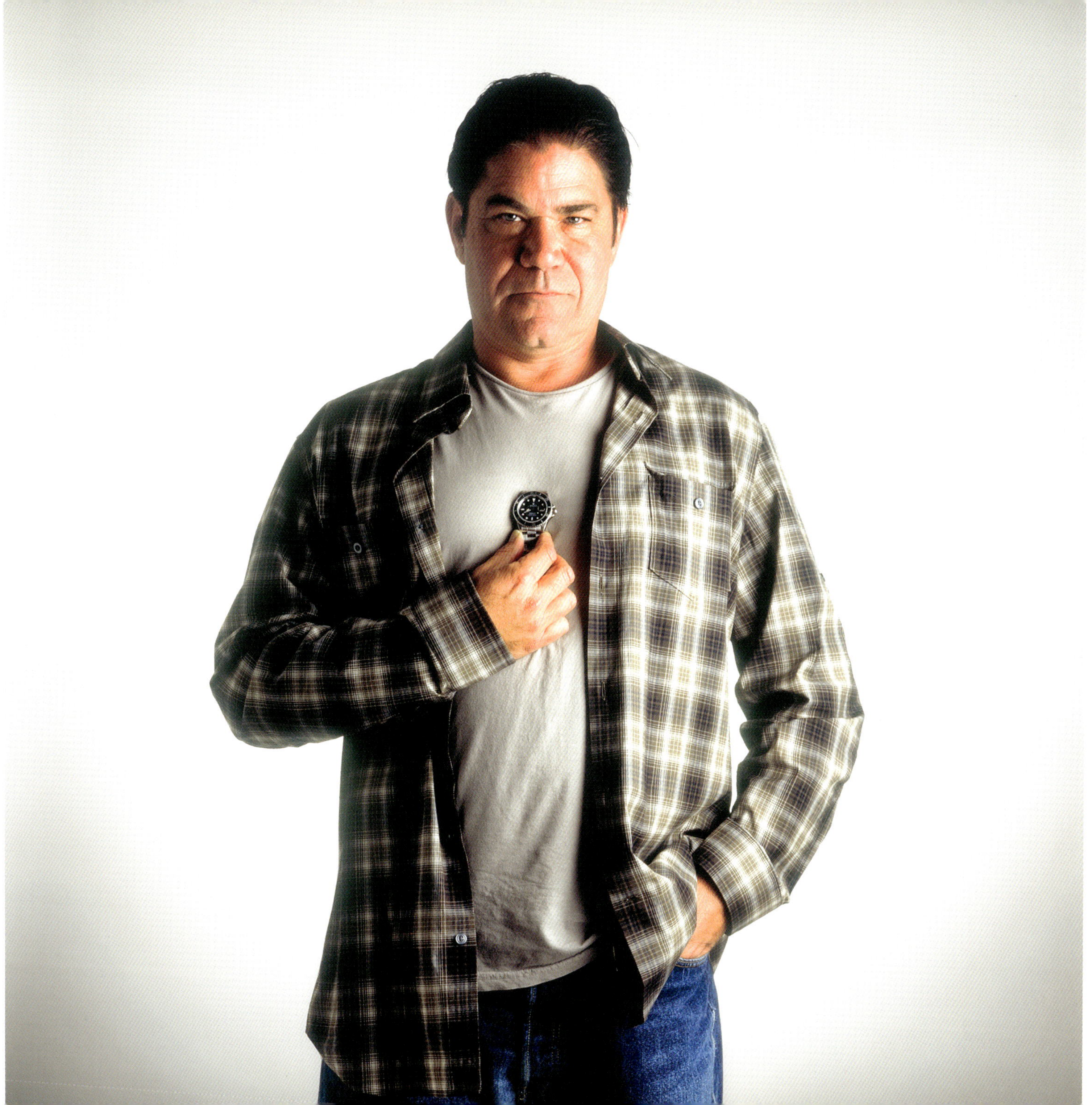

My house is my largest task
By building it I avoided a la
morgage and ~~allowed~~ provide savings to
pay my three daughters ~~cost~~ money for
of college educations

Lee Butler
July 5 2010

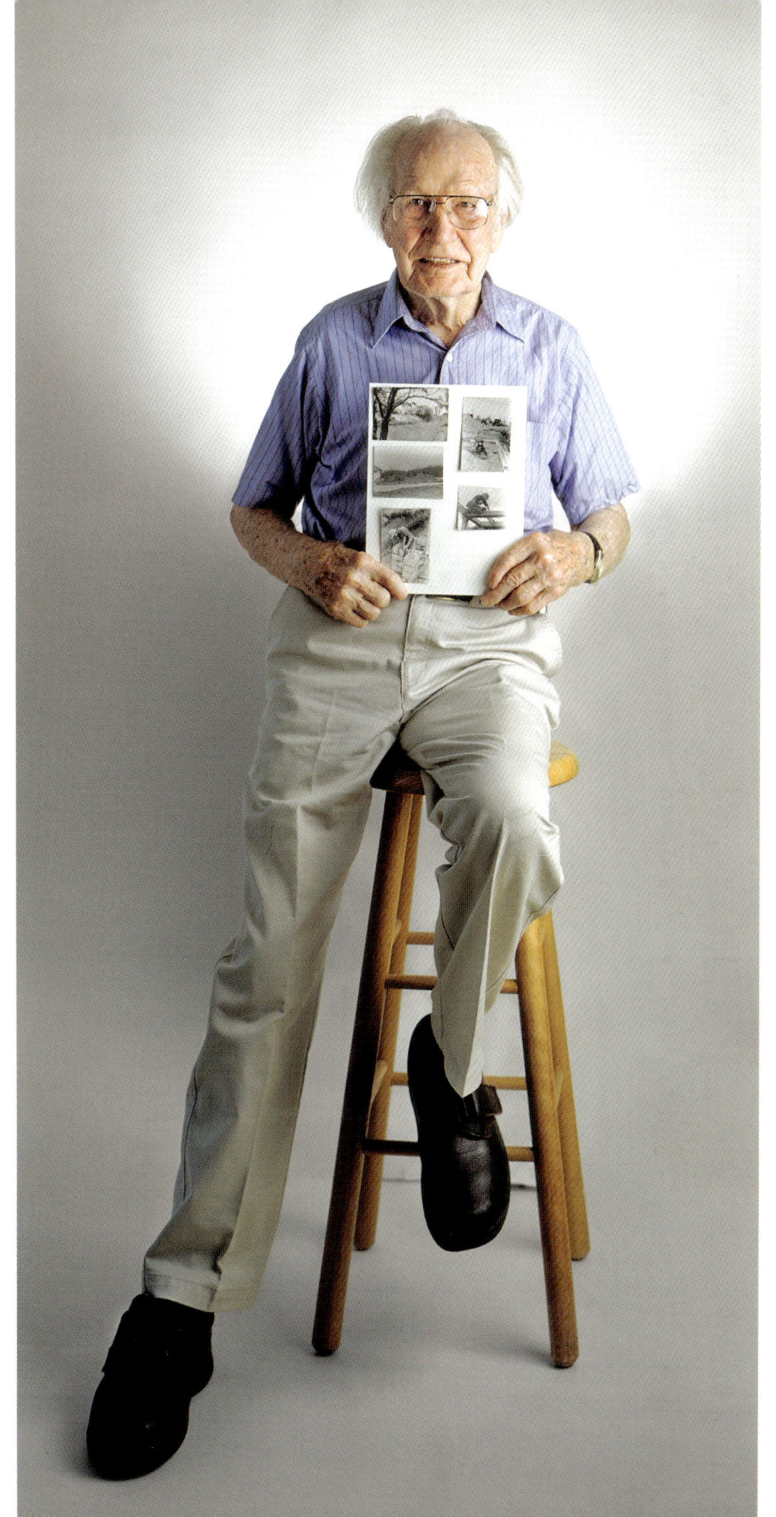

LEO

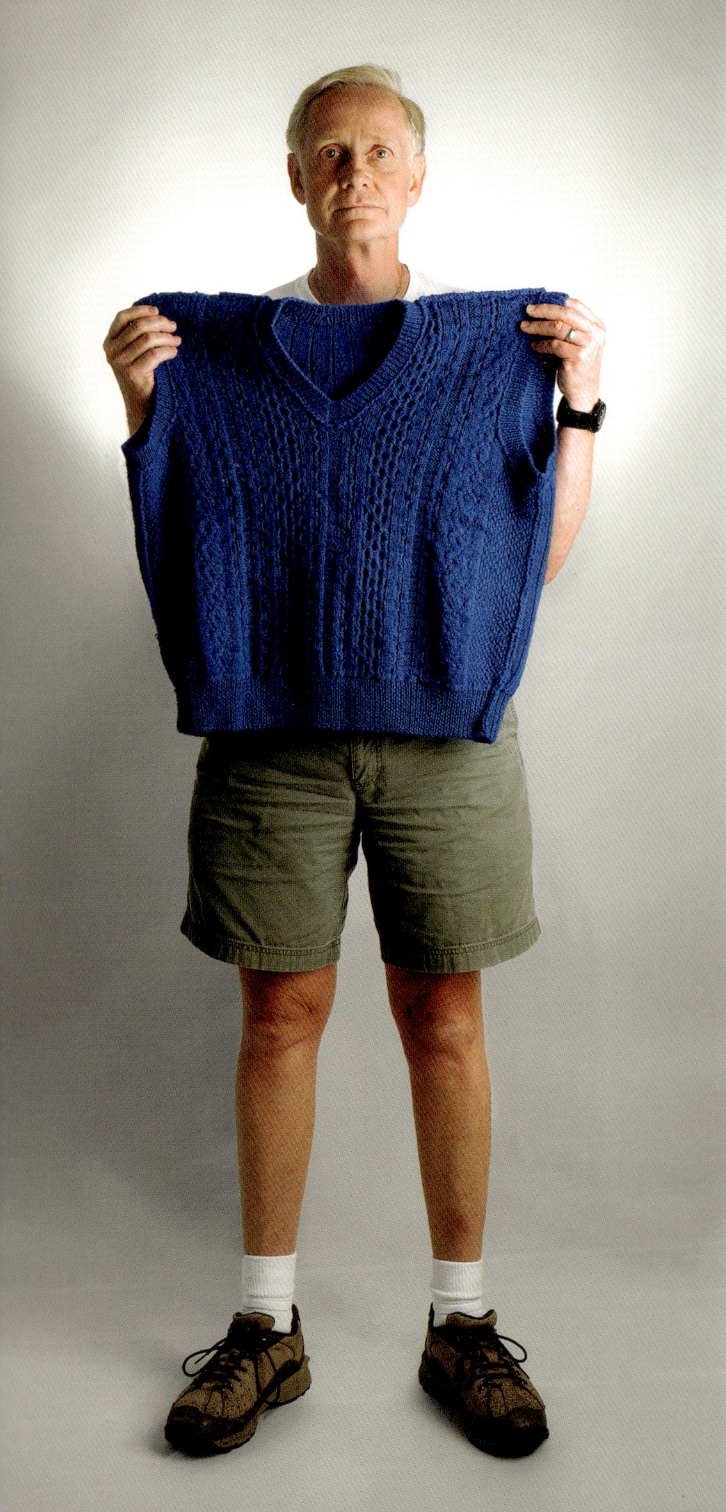

#1. Needle Point

Gift given to me by my Aunt Nisha. She was a holocaust survivor who left Poland and started a new life in Sweden. Her handwritten note in the lower right hand corner is very personal and a great memory of her.

#2. Sweater

Gift of my Aunt Ola - sister of Nisha - also a holocaust survivor. She made the sweater for me but could have picked a calmer color.

Gregory A. Brzozowski

GREG

The watch is in tough shape but still important to me. It belonged to my father's uncle Julius "Schulles" Ernst. Schulles was something of a WWI ace for the Germans. The Nazis urged him to denounce his Jewish wife, my father's Tante Ma, but he refused. The only time I ever saw my father cry was while he was looking at a photo of Schulles and Tante Ma.

JOHN

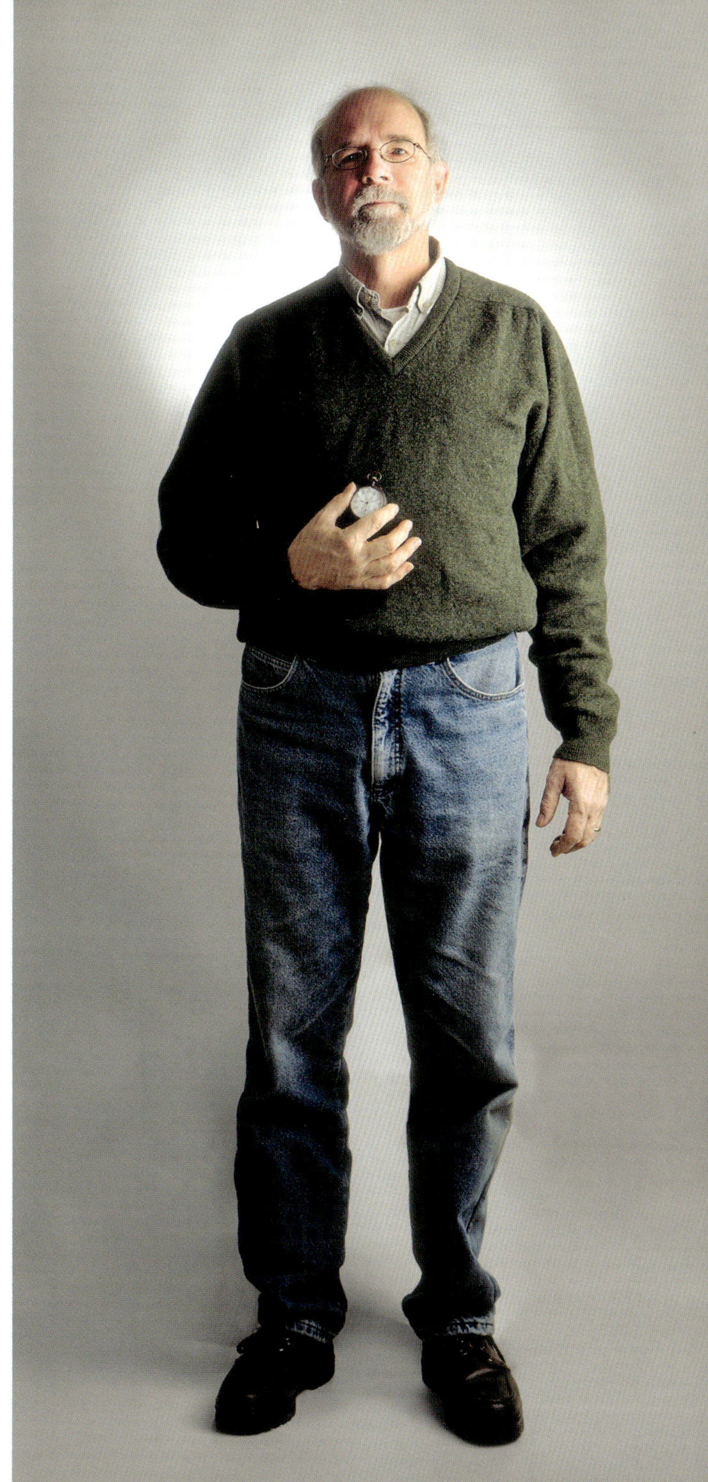

My father, Harold Herman Rosen, was a musician in New York for four decades. As was typical in the first half of the 20th Century, dad went by the professional name of Hal Roland. The microphone delivered his musical talent and great sense of humor to the guests of many bar mitzvahs, weddings, and birthday celebrations on the east coast. Dad would have been 100 years old on November 23, 2010.

Betty Rosen Kahn

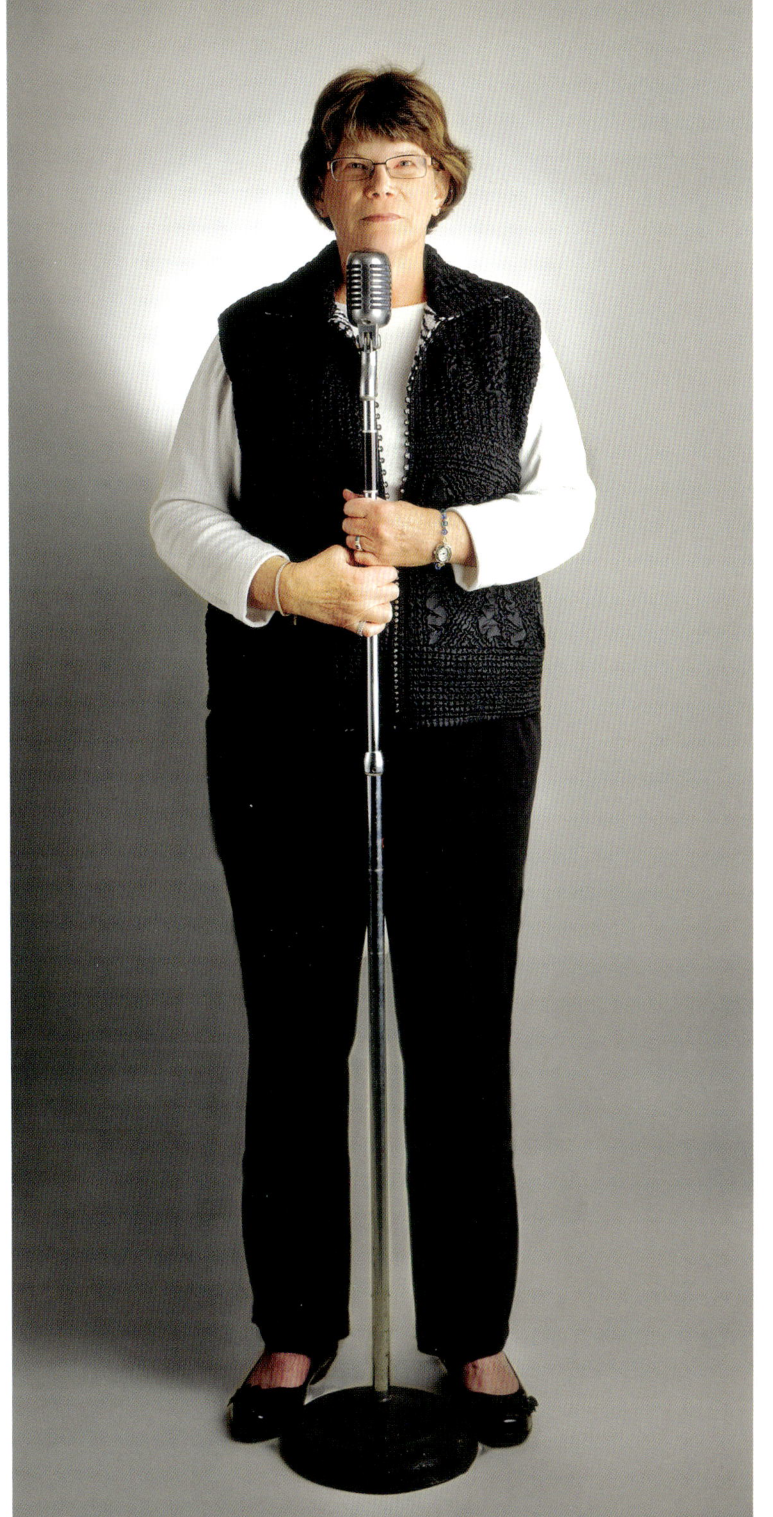

BETTY

IN 1941, THE YEAR MY MOTHER AND HER TWIN WERE BORN, MY PAPA & NANA BOUGHT A MODEST GEORGIAN HOME IN AKRON OHIO. A CRYSTAL CHANDELIER HUNG ABOVE THE DININGROOM TABLE, A TABLE THAT I HAVE IN MY HOME TODAY. MY PRECIOUS OBJECT IS ONE OF THE CRYSTAL PRISMS THAT HUNG FROM IT. I LOVED MY PAPA & NANA DEEPLY. AS A BOY I WOULD PLAY WITH THESE PRISMS WITH OUT PERMISSION. IT WASN'T UNUSUAL FOR A PRISM IS A METAPHOR FOR THE UNCONDITIONAL LOVE THEY GAVE ME & I NOW TRY TO GIVE MY DAUGHTERS.

DANIEL

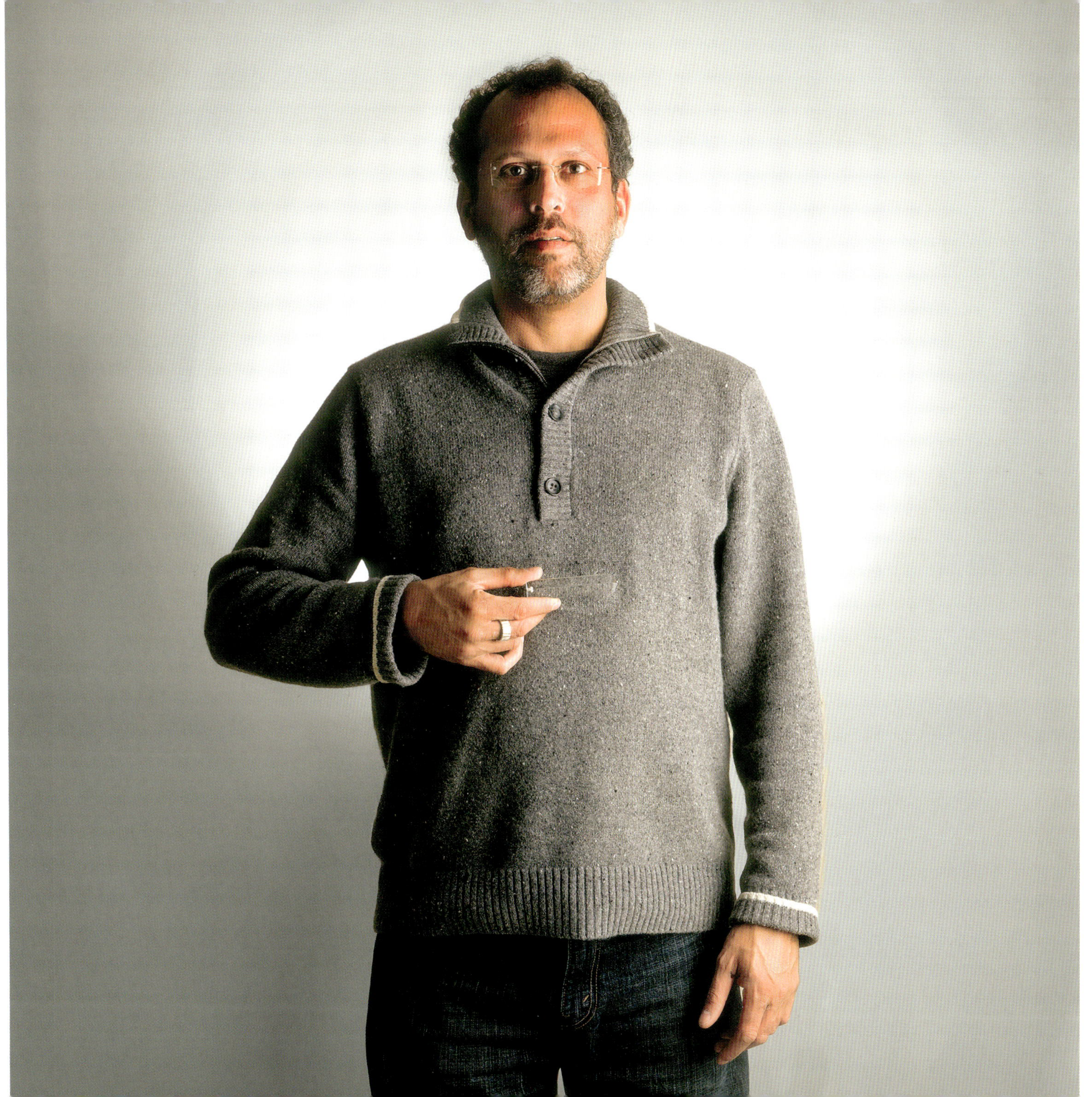

The perfume bottle was the first perfume that I have used during my first dating experience. Inside the bottle is my memory of young, innocent, confusion and obsessing.

Qian Li
1.5.2010

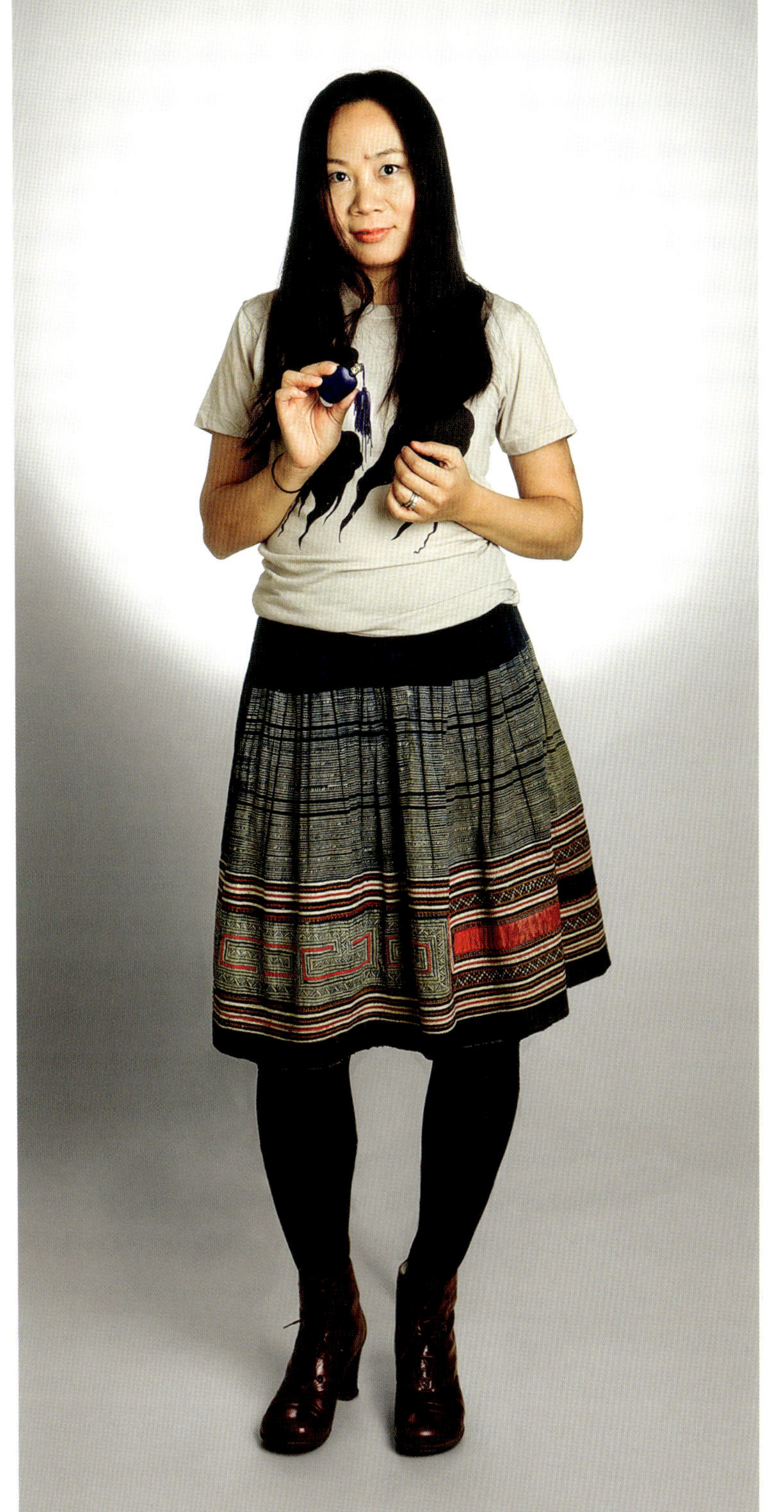

QIAN

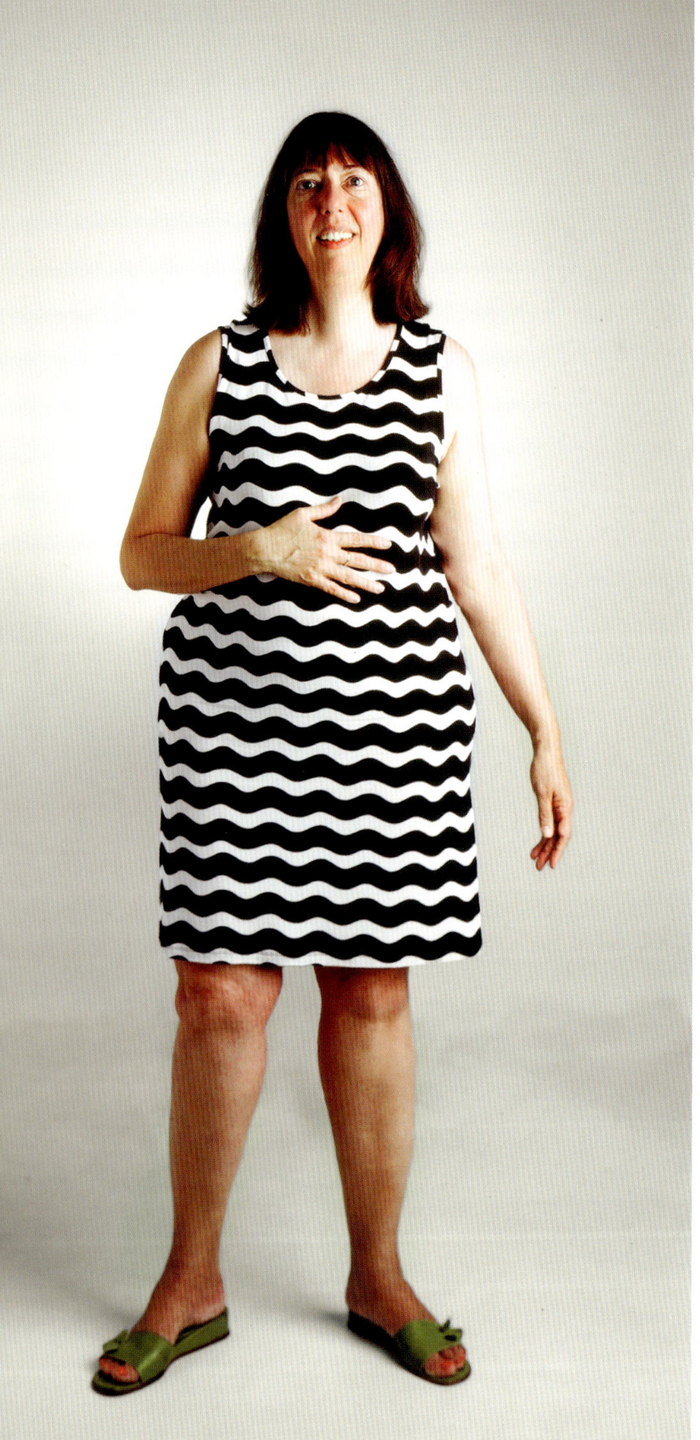

Alison de Lima Greene 8/21/10

On being invited to participate in this project, I immediately volunteered to pose wearing my great grand-mother's wedding ring. The lines of family are very long on my mother's side, so this ring celebrated a wedding that occurred over 130 years ago. The names of my great grandparents – Elias + Esther – is inscribed in Hebrew – they were Sephardim who came to the new world via Curaçao. I like to carry with me this memory of where I came from + this token of love

ALISON

My sister and I share the same birthday. Last year we celebrated together and my parents gave each of us a box as we finished up the cake. A turquoise and gold nest ring and butterfly necklace were cradled inside. The coral pendant and ring were in her box. We looked at each other and mouthed, "Switch"

The objects belonged to our grandmother, Lottie, who passed away several years ago. These objects represent the love my grandparents shared, the unspoken understanding between sisters, and the caring guardianship of parents. Our grandmother's style bended 1950's feminine ideals with Texas practicality. Her will left her granddaughters shotguns and jewelry. They represent tradition, nostalgia and that precious objects remind us to remember our legacy and our roots.

BEVIN

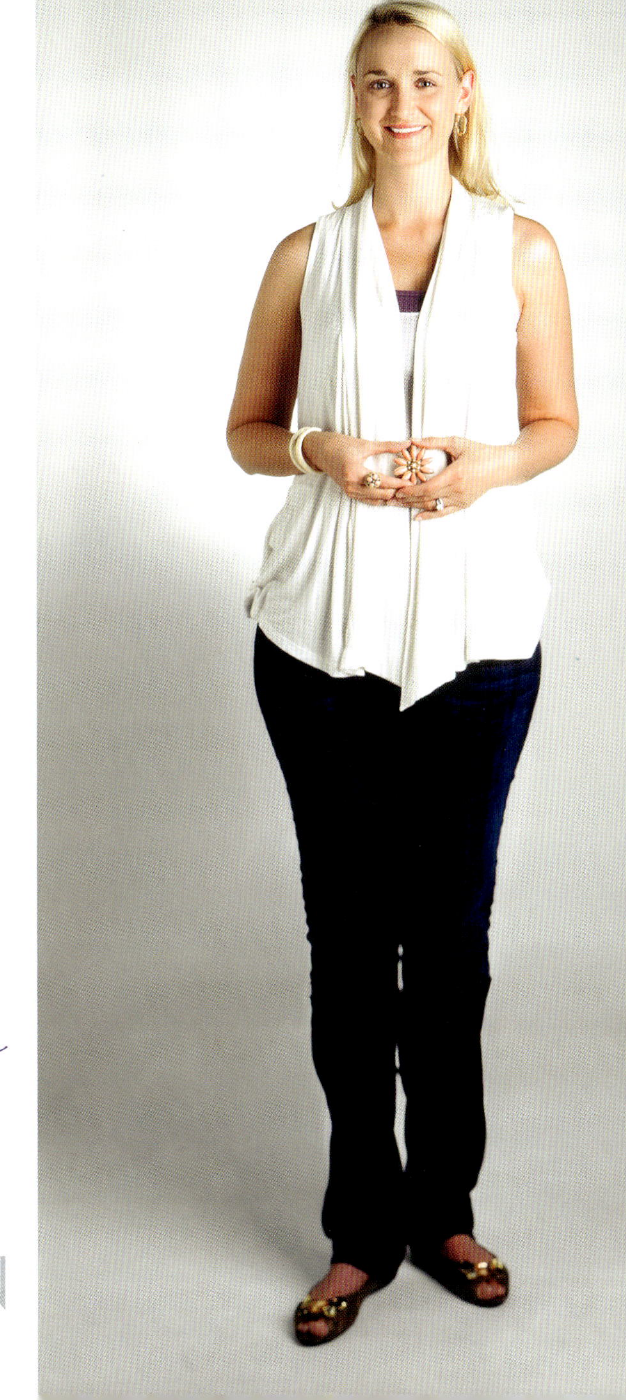

MY FATHER WAS NEVER VERY TALKATIVE SO WHEN HE DIED, I KEPT HIS FALSE TEETH. NOW I KEEP HIS TEETH AND TALK TO HIM EVERY MORNING. HE STILL DOESN'T SAY MUCH BUT I AM HOPEFUL.

– ROBBII

ROBBII

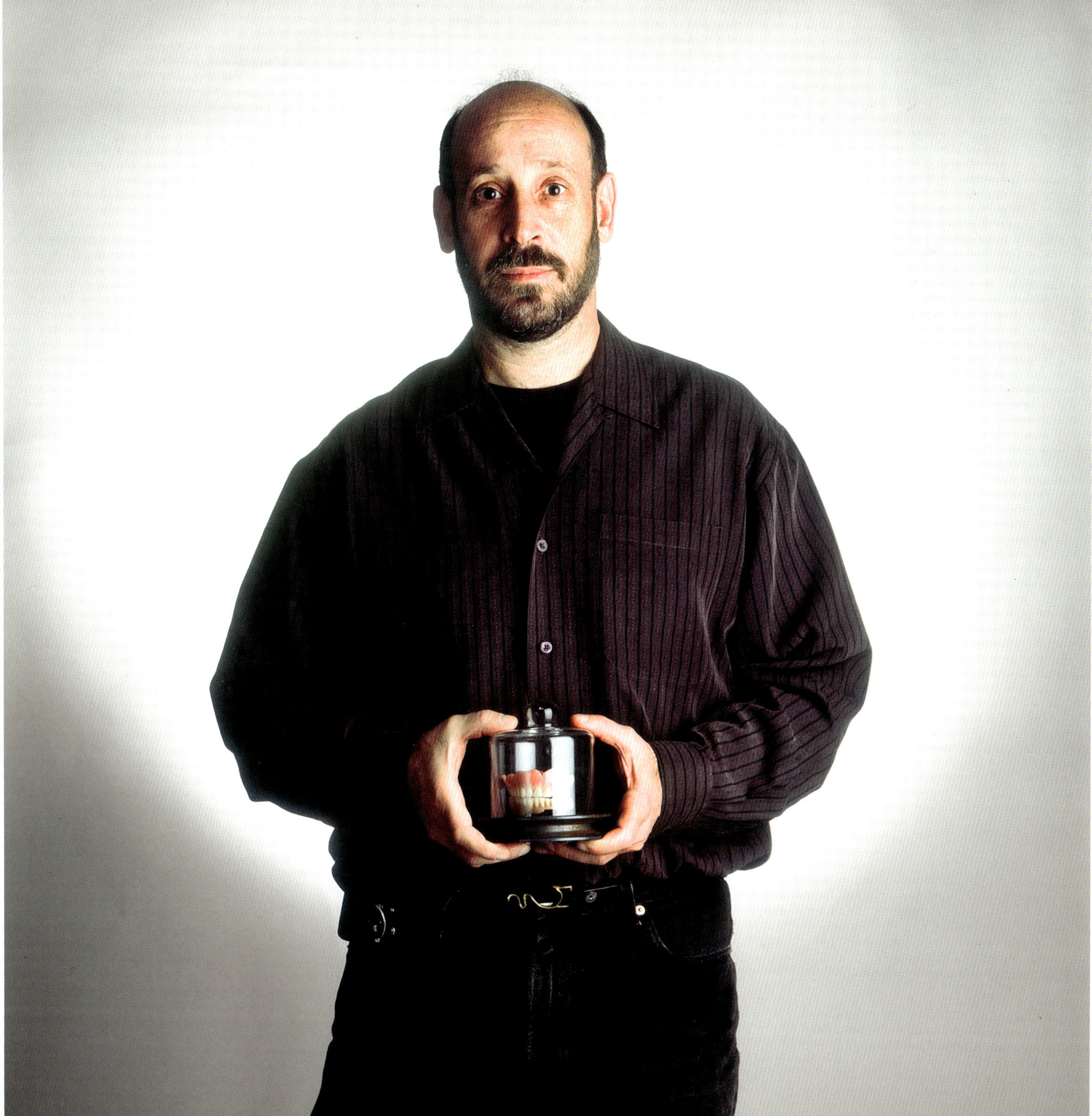

This book is dedicated to all those who participated in *Precious Objects*

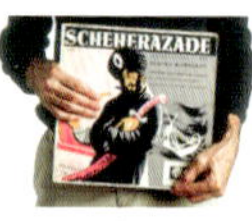

Alan

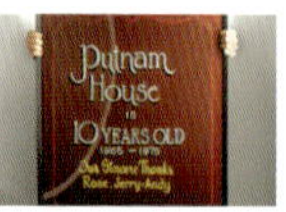

Andy

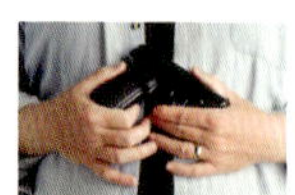
Bob

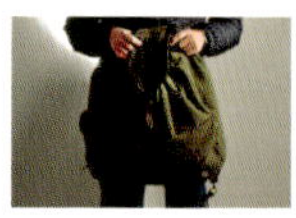
Christian

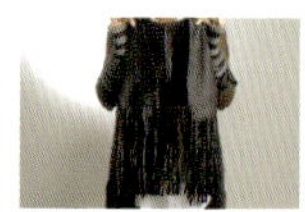
Deb

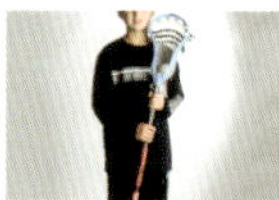
Drew

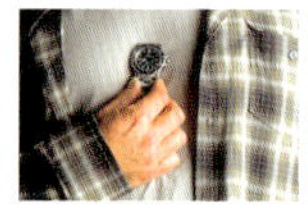
Gary

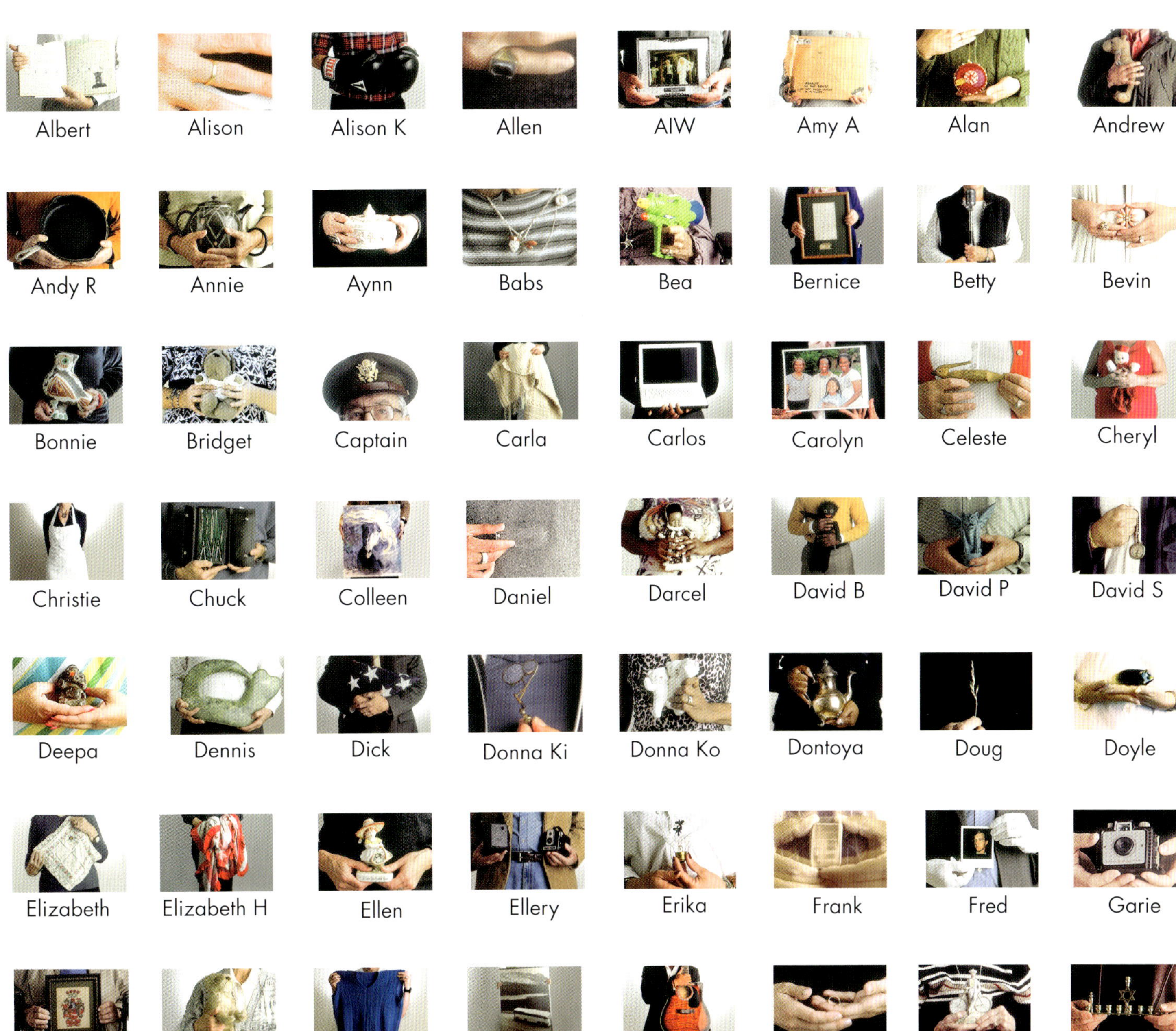

Albert Alison Alison K Allen AIW Amy A Alan Andrew
Andy R Annie Aynn Babs Bea Bernice Betty Bevin
Bonnie Bridget Captain Carla Carlos Carolyn Celeste Cheryl
Christie Chuck Colleen Daniel Darcel David B David P David S
Deepa Dennis Dick Donna Ki Donna Ko Dontoya Doug Doyle
Elizabeth Elizabeth H Ellen Ellery Erika Frank Fred Garie
George Grace Greg Gretchen Harrelson Heidi Helen Herbert

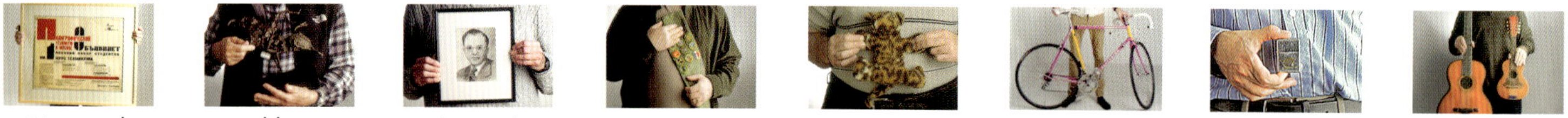

Howard Hy Irwin S Irwin W Isaac Jason Jason C Jeff

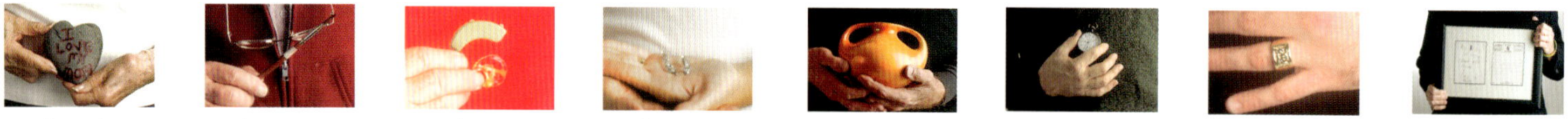

Jennie Jerome Jerry Jessica Jim John C John G John H

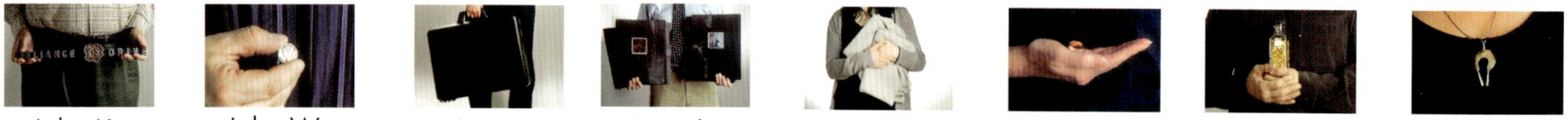

John K John W Jon Joseph Kalli Karen Kathy L Kathy T

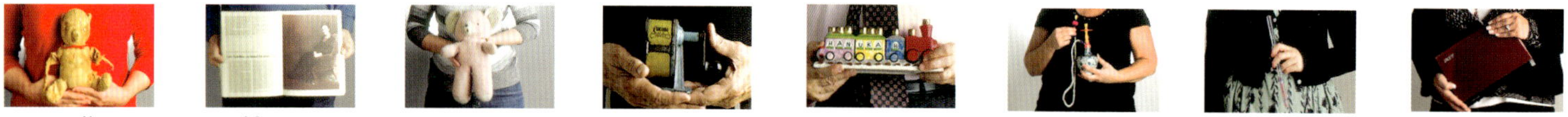

Kelly Kenny Kristina Lane Larry Laura G Laura M Laura S

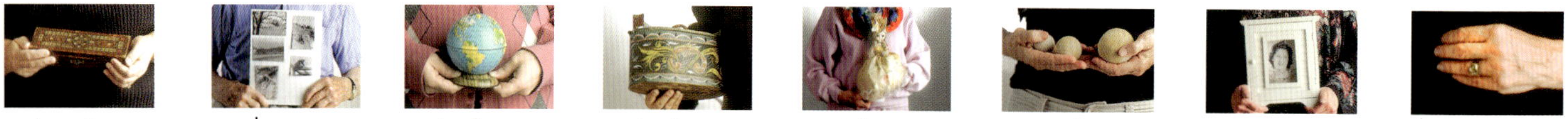

Laurie leo Lesley Leslie Lillian Linda B Linda S Linda Z

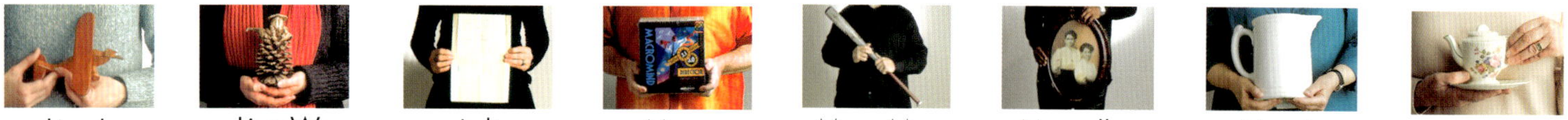

Lisa L Lisa W Loli Marc Marc M Marcellus Marcia Marguerite

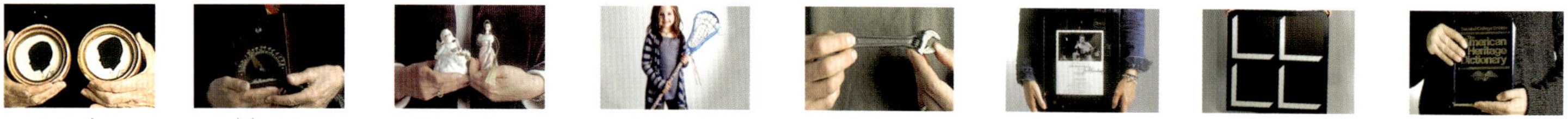

Mark Martin Mary Jane Melanie

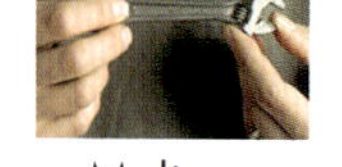

Melissa

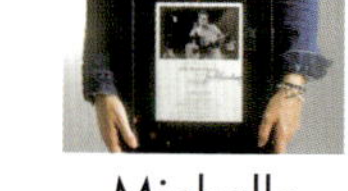

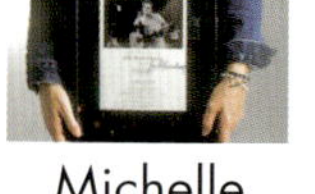

Michelle

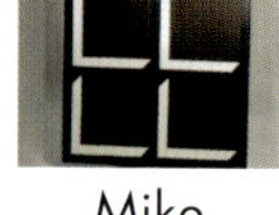

Mike

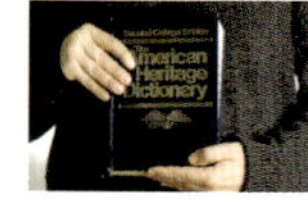

Mike Z

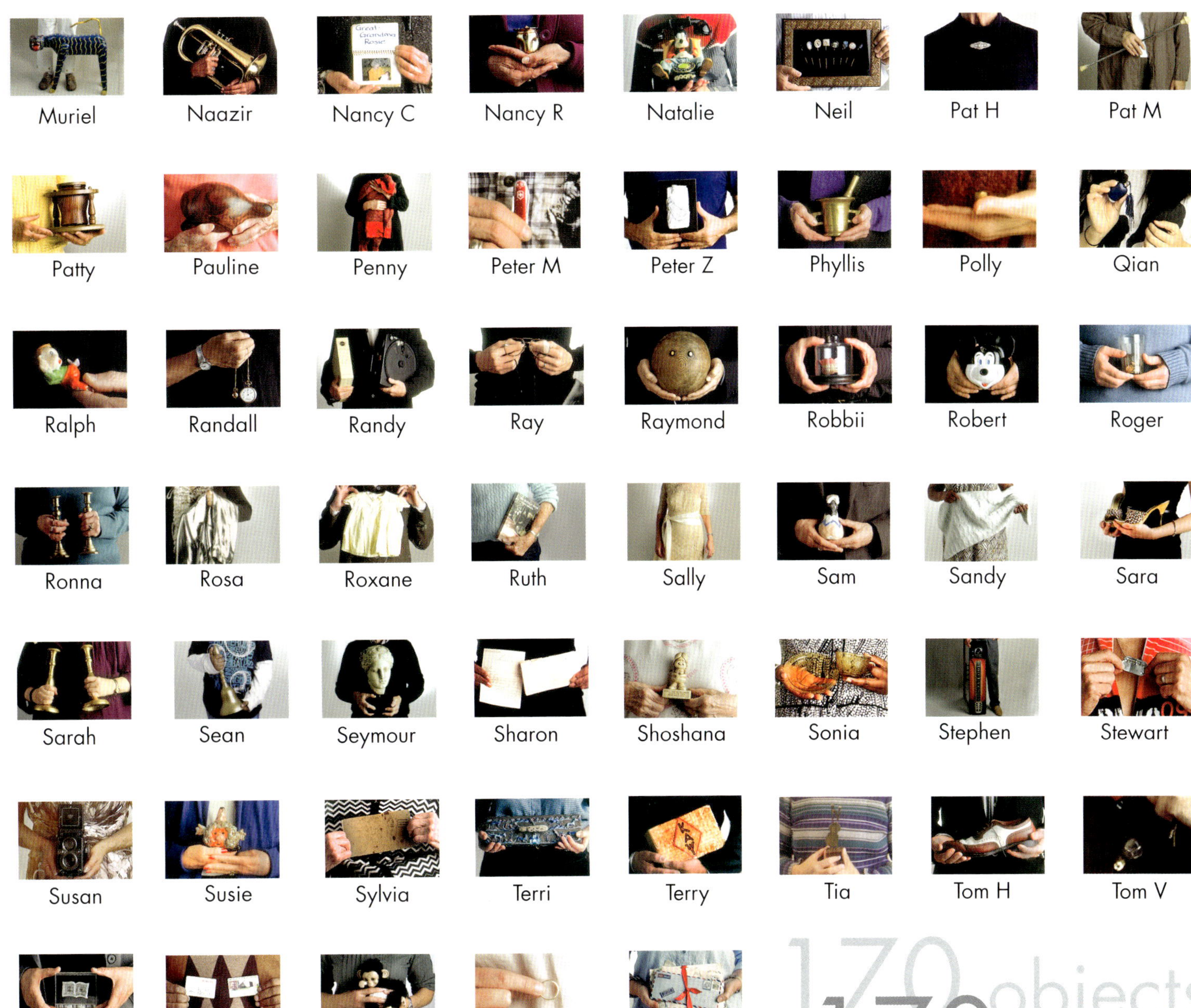

Muriel Naazir Nancy C Nancy R Natalie Neil Pat H Pat M

Patty Pauline Penny Peter M Peter Z Phyllis Polly Qian

Ralph Randall Randy Ray Raymond Robbii Robert Roger

Ronna Rosa Roxane Ruth Sally Sam Sandy Sara

Sarah Sean Seymour Sharon Shoshana Sonia Stephen Stewart

Susan Susie Sylvia Terri Terry Tia Tom H Tom V

Tracey Trevis Vicki Victoria Xavia

170 objects. 170 stories.

MY FATHER BURT, PART OF THE GREATEST GENERATION, DIED IN 2008.

ACKNOWLEDGMENTS

There are a lot of them. Of course, first to all the people who participated, to those who helped me find participants, to those who tried but never came up with the "right" thing and to those who were dragged along with friends or family. To the folks at Houston Center for Photography for making the shoot in Houston possible and to Skyline Studios for allowing me to use their facilities. To Mark at Mason-Murer Gallery in Atlanta for hosting the shoot and to my friend Susan for inviting the entire jazz community. To Laura and the folks at the Long Center for Photography for inviting me and to David at the African-American Museum in Hempstead for hosting the shoot and inviting the community. To my uncle George, of blessed memory, for inviting me to his 90th birthday party and making the LA shoot happen. To my friend Sarah at Stone Gardens that arranged for me to be there and meet the greatest generation. And, of course, to my good friends at the Ohio Historical Society in Columbus who not only hosted *Precious Objects* (and boy do historians love precious objects) but have continued to be partners in my work.

Early in this project, I showed it to some people in Seattle, Crista Dix and Ann Pallesen, who convinced me that sneaking into department stores, as fun as it might be, added nothing and I needed to simplify. Thanks to them.

The folks at CCC, Daniel Levin and Al Wasco, who both participated and recommended my book designer, Leah, deserve special mention as do two other participants, Howard Garfinkel, who put my statement into English and Jon Wilhelm who designed the *Precious Objects* website.

Lastly, a sincere thank you to Spero Smith Financial Services and to the Zanesville Museum of Art for their support in the publishing of this book.

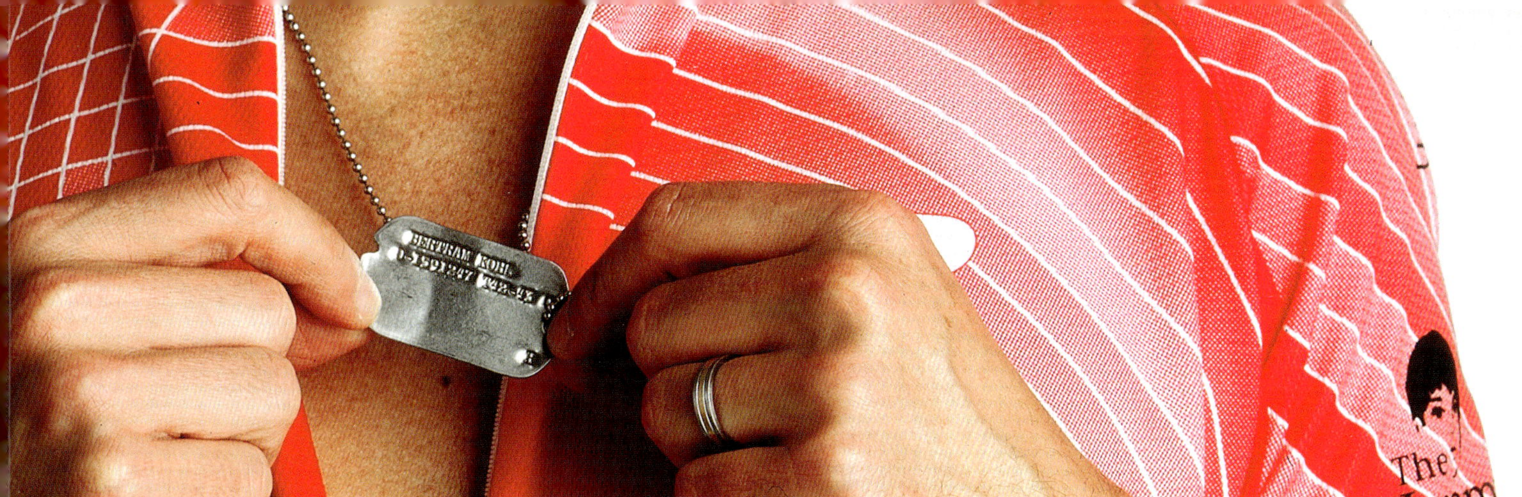

Charles J. Mintz:

Photography is Chuck's third career, the result of a passion acquired in Maine many years ago. Most of his work is done on film. The monochrome is printed in the traditional darkroom, the color scanned and printed on inkjet printers. Although an accomplished Cibachrome printer, he no longer prints color in the darkroom. The experience in color and contrast management strongly affects how he prints digitally.

Becoming full time in 2008 has changed the work in profound ways. Previously, the work showed people anonymously and was more about the public space. In this new time, the work has become intensely personal - often involving portraiture. This can be seen in *The Album Project, Precious Objects* and, still in progress, *Costumes*. Even *Every Place – I Have Ever Lived*, where people in the images are largely unrecognizable, is uniquely personal, beginning with my childhood home that was in foreclosure and continuing in all my lifetime neighborhoods, the work has become less traditionally photographic, both in form and method.

In addition to numerous group and juried exhibitions worldwide, *The Album Project* received a solo exhibition at 1point618 Gallery in 2008. *Every Place – I Have Ever Lived* (the foreclosure crisis in twelve neighborhoods) was installed at the Firelands Association for the Visual Arts in 2011 and at the Ohio Historical Society in 2011-2012. It will be seen at the Argus Museum, in Ann Arbor, Michigan, in September 2012. Chuck also showed his two theater projects at 1point618 Gallery in 2011.

Chuck studied photography at Maine Photographic Workshop, Parsons School of Design, International Center for Photography, Lakeland Community College and Cuyahoga Community College.

He is a director of ICA–Art Conservation in Cleveland, OH and the Cleveland Museum of Art – Friends of Photography. His interest in preservation and conservation is reflected in his service to the ICA and in careful attention to producing work that lasts. Chuck is on the board of WireNet and is a Life Director at Jewish Family Services of Cleveland.

His work can be found in private and corporate collections in North America and Asia.

Chuck is married and lives with his wife in the Detroit Shoreway neighborhood in Cleveland. They have a son, Isaac, and a daughter, Laura. Chuck is an avid cyclist to help offset the fact that he is an avid eater.

For further information visit: www.chuckmintz.com

BOOK DESIGN

Leah Vidosh Peterson
vidoshdesign.com

Precious Objects

Also by Charles J. Mintz: *The Album Project*

Chuck is represented by

1point618 Gallery
Cleveland, Ohio
www.1point618gallery.com

Printed and bound by
AGS Custom Graphics
Cleveland, Ohio

Designed and produced in the
United States of America

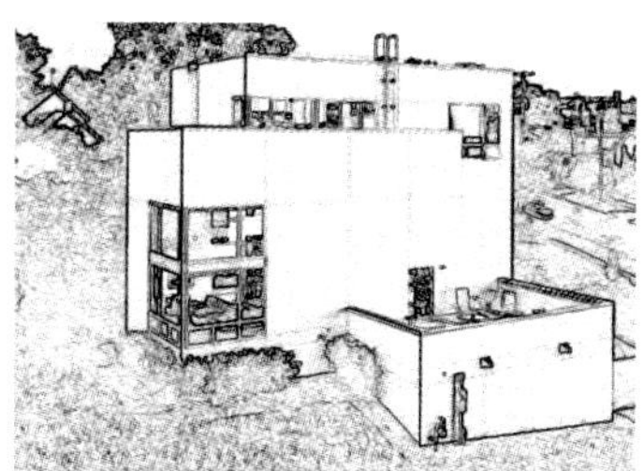

King's Hill Press
www.kingshillpress.com

Front and Back Cover: Isaac

Cover Page
Child's Tea Pot: Marguerite
Picture of Mom: Marcellus
Clay Figure: Susie

Acknowledgments: Stewart